The ABCs of Getting Out of Debt

*Turn Bad Debt into Good Debt
and Bad Credit into Good Credit*

GARRETT SUTTON, ESQ.

The ABCs of Getting Out of Debt

Turn Bad Debt into Good Debt
and Bad Credit into Good Credit

GARRETT SUTTON, ESQ.

Published by BZK Press, LLC

Rich Dad Advisors, B-I Triangle, CASHFLOW Quadrant and other Rich Dad marks are registered trademarks of CASHFLOW Technologies, Inc.

BZK Press LLC
2248 Meridian Blvd.
Suite H
Minden, NV 89423
775-782-2201

Visit our Web sites: BZKPress.com MyBestAdvisors.com

Printed in the United States of America

First Edition: November 2004
First BZK Press Edition: June 2012

ISBN: 978-1-937832-07-0

Acknowledgments

First and foremost, I would like to thank Gerri Detweiler, our contributing editor, for her valuable input, assistance and specialized knowledge, all of which have significantly improved the content of this book. I would like to thank Brandi MacLeod for all her efforts in shaping, reviewing and moving the manuscript forward. As well, I would like to thank Robert and Kim Kiyosaki, Scott Bilker and Tom Quinn for their beneficial thoughts and stories. To all, your contributions are greatly appreciated.

Finally, I would like to thank the producers, directors and prop guys of the Universal Pictures' released film "Wanted," starring Angelina Jolie and Morgan Freeman. Your choice of this book to help shape James McAvoy's character was a brilliant bit of casting.

Best-Selling Books
In the Rich Dad Advisors Series

by Blair Singer

SalesDogs
You Don't Have to Be an Attack Dog to Explode Your Income

Team Code of Honor
The Secrets of Champions in Business and in Life

by Garrett Sutton, Esq.

Start Your Own Corporation
Why the Rich Own Their Own Companies and Everyone Else Works for Them

Writing Winning Business Plans
*How to Prepare a Business Plan that Investors will Want to Read –
and Invest In*

Buying and Selling a Business
How You Can Win in the Business Quadrant

The ABCs of Getting Out of Debt
Turn Bad Debt into Good Debt and Bad Credit into Good Credit

Run Your Own Corporation
*How to Legally Operate and Properly Maintain Your Company
into the Future*

The Loopholes of Real Estate
Secrets of Successful Real Estate Investing

by Ken McElroy

The ABCs of Real Estate Investing
The Secrets of Finding Hidden Profits Most Investors Miss

The ABCs of Property Management
What You Need to Know to Maximize Your Money Now

The Advanced Guide to Real Estate Investing
How to Identify the Hottest Markets and Secure the Best Deals

by Tom Wheelwright

Tax-Free Wealth
How to Build Massive Wealth by Permanently Lowering Your Taxes

Contents

Foreword
by Robert Kiyosaki

I Love My Credit Cards

In the late 1980's, I went to a seminar on financial success. The instructor, a young charismatic speaker, went on and on about the perils of debt, saying repeatedly, "Debt is bad. Debt is your enemy. Get out of debt as soon as you can." Looking around the room at approximately fifty attendees, I could see most heads were nodding in agreement.

Just before the break, the young speaker asked, "Okay, are you ready to cut your ties with the bondage of debt?" Most attendees nodded. "If you are ready to break the bonds, then stand, get out your credit cards, and hold them up high so everyone in the room can see them." Most of the class stood immediately while there were several people, like me, who were looking around waiting to see if we should follow or not. Slowly, everyone stood, myself included. I figured that since I had paid money and invested this much time, I might as well go along with the process to see what I could learn. As I held my gold credit card in front of me, a smiling assistant handed me a pair of scissors. As I grasped the scissors, I knew what was to happen next. "Okay, class, cut your credit cards in half," said the instructor. As I heard the sounds of scissors cutting through plastic, there were actually several cries of shock, some groans, and even a few people crying. After cutting my card in half, I just stood in silence, mostly numb, waiting for some form of educated enlightenment to sweep over me. Nothing happened. I just felt numb. Although I had been in credit card trouble in the late 1970's, when my nylon and Velcro wallet business was caving in on me, I did eventually clean up my debt and had gone on to use my credit cards more responsibly; hence I did not have the same cathartic reaction some people in the class seemed to have when they cut their cards in half.

In less than a week, my replacement card had arrived in the mail and I was happily on my way, using my gold card again. Although I did not have a blinding cognition after cutting my credit card, the process did make me more aware of how much of a problem credit, primarily its use and abuse, can be in a persons' life. Today I watch many so-called financial experts saying the same things that young instructor was saying years ago, such things as "Get out of debt." "Cut up your credit cards." "Put your credit cards in the freezer." The problem I have with much of their advice is that they tend to blame the credit card as the problem, rather than the lack of financial control and financial education of the card user. Blaming one's credit card for their financial woes is much the same as me blaming my putter for my high golf score.

Credit and debt are very important subjects in anyone's life. Today, young people while still in school are actively solicited by credit card companies, which have often caused me to ask, why don't we teach young people about money in school? Why do we have to wait till young people are deeply in credit card debt and in debt due to school loans before we realize there is a problem? If you ask most young people, "What is the difference between *credit and debt*?" I doubt many could tell you the difference, and yet we let financial profiteers educate our youth.

Consumer debt has exploded in the United States and in countries around the world. In 1990, the U.S. consumer was $200 billion deep in credit card debt. In 2008 it rose to over $957 billion, and has now adjusted downward to over $800 billion, a huge number nevertheless. That does not include the national debt – the U.S. is the largest debtor nation in the world – nor the debt many financial institutions have exposure to worldwide. As we have learned, you can't extend easy credit forever. When the world calls its loans, when people and organizations are not able to pay their bills and credit becomes tight, huge financial problems surface, which ultimately affect our individual credit card balances.

So are debt and credit bad, as so many financial experts say? Absolutely not. Debt and credit are powerful financial tools that have allowed many in the world to enjoy the highest standard of living in history. Without debt and credit, we would not have such things as great cities, massive industries, airlines flying us to all parts of the world, resorts to relax at, excellent food at exciting restaurants, new cars to drive, comfortable homes to live in, and so many choices of entertainment.

So if debt and credit are not bad, then what is? In my opinion, lack of financial education and fiscal responsibility are bad. I think it tragic that my parents' generation, the World War II generation, has left massive debt for my generation; and my generation, the Vietnam era generation, has done the same to our kids. In other words, while personal credit card abuse is irresponsible, the massive bill each generation passes on to the next generation is even more irresponsible.

How young people born in the new millennium will pay for multiple generations of fiscal irresponsibility, I do not know. One way to keep paying for all this debt is to keep expanding credit and encouraging people to spend more and more. The June 28, 2004, issue of *Time* magazine ran an article about schools now sending kids on field trips to shopping malls, car dealerships, supermarkets, and fast-food outlets. Why? One reason is that our cash-strapped schools cannot afford to send kids on field trips to zoos, museums, or cultural events. Yet many businesses are ready and willing to pay for these field trips to start grooming new customers while they are still in school. In other words, as long as each of us keeps consuming and keeps using our credit to acquire more debt, the economy will grow and the bills of past generations will be paid. While this may be good for business and will help keep our credit and debt economy afloat, to me it sounds risky and fiscally irresponsible.

The good news is that even though most of us cannot control our national irresponsibility, we can take control of our own finances. One of the most important lessons my rich dad taught me was the wisdom of knowing there is good debt and bad debt. Simply put, rich dad said,

"Good debt makes you rich and bad debt makes you poor." Unfortunately, most of the people who were cutting up their credit cards in the financial seminar I attended only had bad debt. Even more unfortunate was that the instructor leading the class only knew of bad debt. He had no idea that good debt existed. To him, all debt was bad. Bad financial education is the cause of poor financial management.

One of the reasons this book is so important is that it is important to be financially responsible and to use the power of your credit and debt intelligently. Before turning you loose into this book, I would like to pass on three bits of information my rich dad taught me years ago. They are:

1. *Bad debt is easier to get than good debt.* If any of you have ever tried to get a loan to buy a rental property or to start a business, you may know how difficult it is to get a loan for investment. Yet if you want a car loan or a new credit card, credit, debt, and money are easy to come by, even if you have horrible credit.

2. *Bad debt makes it harder to get good debt.* If you have too much bad debt, and you want to begin using the power of debt and credit more intelligently, like for starting a business or investing in rental property, bad debt makes it harder for you to get the good debt and hence to become richer. One big reason this book is so important is that getting rid of your bad debt is an important step toward you becoming richer and more financially free.

3. *Debtors can get rich faster than savers.* Many people think that saving is better than borrowing. In fact, I know that many people work hard to save money and get out of debt. In reality, it is those who save and get out of debt who fall behind those that borrow and get into debt.

Let me use an example to explain this last statement. In 2002, my wife, Kim, purchased a commercial building for approximately $8 million. She put $1 million down and borrowed $7 million dollars. The million-dollar down payment came from accrued gains in her other investments, so technically, the $8 million purchase was a nothing down investment.

This investment alone puts approximately $30,000 a month in her pocket. While many people do not make $30,000 a year, her private company makes this in a month.

To people who are savers and debt averse, I often ask them, "How long would it take you to save $7 million?" For most people, saving $7 million is out of their reality. I then ask Kim how long it took her to borrow $7 million. Her reply is, "It took me about two weeks. Because it was such a great real estate investment, several bankers wanted to give me the money."

That is an example explaining why a debtor can get rich faster than a saver. Not only is the debtor getting richer, but the saver is getting poorer. Due to inflation and the irresponsible printing of more and more money, your dollars in savings are going down in value each year, while the debtor's property is often going up in value. A person who saves loses as the debtors who invest in real estate win.

The reason Garrett Sutton's book is so important is that, like it or not, debt is a powerful force in our world today. The financially intelligent are using debt to enrich themselves while the financially uneducated or irresponsible are using debt to destroy their lives. There is good debt and bad debt in this world. A very important lesson in one's life is to know how to minimize bad debt and responsibly use good debt to one's advantage. This is especially true in today's financially changing world.

Years ago, after cutting up my credit card, I realized how important my rich dad's lessons on debt and credit have been to me. That day, in the seminar, I realized that many of the participants should have cut up their credit cards. But cutting up your credit cards will not necessarily make you richer. A credit card is a very powerful tool, and that is why I love my credit card because I would rather have its power than be without its power. For a more enriched life, one must learn to respect the power of debt and credit, and learn how to use that power.

Robert Kiyosaki

Part One

Credit and Debt

Chapter One

An Introduction to the Credit System

Fighting for a Chance

Donny protected his country. As a firefighter trained to fight large forest fires he was sent around the country to protect people and property from the forces of nature. Americans could go about their daily business, could sleep safe at night with their families because of Donny and his fire-fighting unit, experts at fighting wild fires, preserving forests and family homes. He felt satisfaction in knowing what he did mattered.

Donny was a recent college graduate. Like over a third of all college graduates he had student loan debts; in his case over $20,000 was due. Like over half of all college students, he had more than two credit cards with an unpaid balance of over $2,000 each. In Donny's case the total was $4,500. His first card had been burdened with charges to impress a worthy co-ed. The relationship didn't last. The debt did. His second card was from a national department store chain. He received 10% off everything in the store when he applied for the card. He was still paying off several of the shirts he no longer wore.

Donny had recently financed the purchase of a new Ford F150. It was a great truck he needed to have. He was certain he could make all of the payments. The local fire department paid him like clock work.

Donny was sent to fight a huge summer fire in Oregon. Another mission, another job to do. In the past, when on the fire lines, Donny had always been able to receive his bills and make payments on a timely basis.

Then a white powder was found on an envelope at his local post office. It was anthrax. The post office was shut for three weeks while the matter was carefully investigated. The mail didn't move for another six weeks.

Donny didn't receive his bills. Meanwhile, the Oregon wild fire threatened towns and property in all directions. He was on the lines for seemingly the entire summer. Like all of the other firefighters in his unit, he assumed that the creditors were aware of the situation and would arrange a grace period for payment. After all, they were serving their country.

But the creditors didn't care what Donny was doing. He was now two payments late on all of his bills. That was all that mattered. Explanations, whether reasonable, justified or good, were just excuses. And all excuses were bad.

Donny's credit card had a Universal Default Clause, one of the most odious of all credit traps, and one that was restricted later by the Credit CARD Act – too late to help Donny. By being one day late on any payment to any creditor, the credit card company could charge a default rate on any existing balance of up to 29.99%. This meant that in Donny's case he had to pay an extra $2,500 a year for being one month late on another creditor's bill.

Donny missed two car payments while fighting the huge Oregon fire and the F-150 was repossessed. Because he had just purchased it, the money owed far exceeded the artificially low value it was sold for at auction.

Finally the horrendous Oregon wild fire was brought under control. Donny and scores of other firefighters returned home from a very difficult mission. In gratitude, the country's financial establishment unleashed a torrent of debt collection sharks on the returning heroes.

The firefighters were incensed. They had served their country. Through no fault of their own the mail had been delayed. Under such circumstances a little leeway was appropriate. If they were in the military, the Service Members Civil Relief Act could have shielded them from credit sharks. Why shouldn't firefighters be equally protected? But the creditors didn't care. They had rules and standards. And they made a great deal of money when people paid late. Some of the firefighters were now being forced into bankruptcy. Others lost their homes; many had their futures seriously delayed. A number of them wrote their Congressmen demanding relief from the ingratitude of the nation's credit establishment. But individual firefighters didn't contribute to Congress.

And yet the credit card companies, leasing companies, banks and other lenders spent millions and millions of dollars to influence Congress. There was no contest.

Donny was forced to declare bankruptcy. The next seven years felt like financial hell. He had a black mark on his record he worried about and worked every day to overcome. He had trouble getting approved for more credit, and when he did, he paid higher rates.

All for the privilege of serving his country.

Playing the Credit Game

Dewey liked to play the angles. If there was an opportunity for him to take advantage of a situation or of someone else he would do so. Especially if it meant easy money without the need for work.

Recently, Dewey had turned to new credit card and bank account deals. The FBI called it identity theft, and claimed it was the fastest growing crime in America. Dewey preferred to call it selective borrowing, and it was so easy and so lucrative he'd wished he known about it sooner.

Dewey had learned that by obtaining someone's social security number along with basic personal information he could obtain a credit card and a bank account. The accounts would be in the unsuspecting person's name but available for the use and benefit of Dewey, who moved from city to city to ply his special talents.

Dewey had just obtained the personal information from an elderly gentleman named John Logan. It was all so easy. He called up Mr. Logan pretending to be a utility company representative. He said he needed the information to update the company's files. Mr. Logan was all too nice and willing and forthcoming.

Dewey's friend could forge a driver's license to perfection. His friend's business used to be geared toward underaged teens who wanted to go bar hopping. The market now was for sharpies like Dewey. With Dewey's photo and driver's license carrying John Logan's information and an address controlled by Dewey, the plan was put in motion. Dewey opened a bank account in John Logan's name. He paid a few small bills and maintained good credit for a time. Then Dewey obtained a credit card in Logan's name. All was ready to prime the credit pump.

With the credit card Dewey bought as much electronics as the card would allow. TVs, stereos and computers were easily fenced for cash. Dewey felt no remorse. The credit card companies and the national electronics retail chain made more than enough money. They could easily afford Dewey's hit. So could old Mr. Logan for that matter.

With his bank account Dewey wrote a large number of checks on one weekend to a number of small retail outlets around town. The smaller stores didn't have the ability to check cash availability. It was the weekend. The banks were closed. They took down John Logan's driver's license information and Dewey loaded up a rental U-Haul truck with his purchases.

By the time the checks started bouncing, Dewey was hundreds of miles away getting ready for his next selective borrowing.

Unlike the credit card charges, which were absorbed by the credit card company and passed onto consumers around the world in the form of higher prices, the small retailers Dewey hit were not so lucky. When the bounced checks came back the retailer was responsible. They were out the money they paid for the goods they handed over to Dewey.

The scam also cost the John Logan's of the world dearly. Calls from the creditors and collection agencies, even when one is innocent, takes its toll. The crushing financial and resulting emotional stress of a stolen identity is too much for many to take. For John Logan, a stroke followed. He died shortly thereafter.

The stories of Donny and Dewey illustrate the extremes and the ironies of credit and debit problems facing so many Americans.

The credit industry actively entices all comers, especially the young and inexperienced, with the promise of credit. Critics charge their aggressive practices border on predatory lending, taking unfair advantage of those who shouldn't be borrowing. Whatever the case, the easy availability of credit encourages two types of people to sign up who shouldn't: those represented by Donny and those represented by Dewey.

Donny, fresh from college with student loans, two credit cards and a truck payment, is starting his career on the edge of the credit abyss. If he doesn't work, he is in trouble. Dewey, always ready to play the angles, has found a career taking advantage of the credit industries' willingness to lend, allowing him to work causing trouble. To combat the Deweys of the world, the credit industry responds with rules and a rigidity that move the Donnys closer to the abyss. One missed payment, anytime, for any reason, be it anthrax or cows in the road slowing the mail, and the machinery of negative credit can start to grind. A freefall ensues. A number of lives are ruined.

The irony of this scenario is how the credit industry treats each individual. Dewey is a cost of doing business. His fraud is known and accounted in their budgets is an expense factor. The cost is spread out over the entire industry with millions and millions of consumers footing the bill as increased costs.

Donny, on the other hand, the deserving and ethical individual and a victim of circumstance, is a casualty of doing business. He had his chance, argue industry experts, and he missed a payment. He will be punished until he can be trusted once again.

And so in this upside down world where criminality is a cost and inadvertence amounts to a crime, it is important to know the rules, the motivations and the road map for winning with credit.

First, let's look at what motivates us to get into debt...

Chapter Two

The Psychology of Debt

Before tackling the rules of debt and how to win with credit it is important to understand the psychology of debt. What are the motivations that lead to debt? Why are some people consistently unable to manage debt? What is the relationship between self-esteem and debt?

With nearly trillions in unpaid consumer debt, a million households filing for bankruptcy each year (more or less, depending on the year), and a very low savings rate, why are we racking up debt like there is no tomorrow?

In my experience there are five types of borrower profiles:

Wishers
Wasters
Wanters
Whiners
Winners

The first three profiles tend to overlap, as we'll see. The last profile, the winners, have either survived and moved past the difficulties of the first four categories, or were credit winners to begin with. This book will teach you how to be a credit winner.

Wishers

Wishers are credit optimists. They have the sunny perception that they deserve the good things; that they are meant to keep up with the Joneses, and can easily afford it all. In their happy dream world of credit optimism they focus on the monthly payments, not on the overall debt. They see a $20 payment here and a $75 payment there as doable, never focusing on the thousands of dollars of overall debt, at crushing interest rates, they have incurred. They are convinced that they can easily pay the bills as they come due.

Such false perceptions of what can be managed are extremely problematic during the Christmas spending season, especially with the sense that the bills are due next year. Wishers, as optimists, see a brighter next year for themselves, a better job, with more income, a future whereby all money issues will be resolved.

Unfortunately, not all wishes come true.

Wasters

Wasters spend money as an escape. With low self esteem issues, they use money to purchase things in order to feel better, relieve stress and escape their problems. In a society where massive and pervasive advertising can easily manipulate behavior, there is nothing like the feel and sense of something new (or so the advertisers would have you believe.) A new car or truck or television or vacation can end the emptiness inside – for a time. When that empty feeling returns there are still bills to pay.

Wasters, however, will continue spending. With a credit card industry that encourages, indeed programs, people to buy now (for wasters – feel now) and pay later, wasters will sign up for more credit. They will find themselves locked into a life of revolving debt. With low self-esteem they will more often declare bankruptcy and they will more often go back to their unsuccessful money management techniques of short-term retail relief and long-term debt woes.

Wanters

One of the more interesting studies in annuals of psychology is the Stanford Marshmallow Study. Begun in the 1960s, it was conducted by

Walter Mischel, a Stanford University psychology researcher, and studied the importance of self-discipline on future success.

A group of hungry 4-year olds was offered a choice. They could have one marshmallow now. But if they waited fifteen or twenty minutes while the researcher ran an errand they could have two marshmallows.

A third of the children immediately ate the single marshmallow. While some waited a little longer, another third of the children waited the full 15 to 20 minutes for the adult to return.

Later, when the children graduated from high school, a follow up study provided interesting information. The quick and single marshmallow eaters were less self-confident and couldn't put off immediate gratification to reach long-term goals. Their impulses were life long, resulting in bad marriages, low job satisfaction and lower incomes.

The resisters, who delayed immediate gratification to receive two marshmallows, were more productive and positive in life. By being able to delay gratification in pursuit of their goals they had higher incomes, more lasting marriages and better health.

The problem in our society is that immediate gratification is actively encouraged. "Have it your way." Eye glasses - or whatever - in under an hour. "Buy now, pay later." These are just some of the constant messages we receive. Is it any wonder that those with lower self-discipline are lured into the indulgences of immediate gratification?

The wanters want it now and the credit industry caters to that desire. The issue of paying for all of it later inevitably becomes a problem.

Whiners

Whiners will start to read this book and will give up because they decide it's too hard, or it won't work, or the deck is stacked against them. They may read lots and lots of information about credit and personal finance but instead of taking action, they continue to spend their time focused on the negative. When a solution or answer is presented to them, they will go into detail about what's wrong with it.

Whiners may rail against FICO, creditors, the banks – or all three. While they may have legitimate concerns about the fairness of the credit system, they spend all their time trying to fight the system, rather than working toward a solution.

Winners

Believe it or not, for all the criticism of the credit industry we have just offered, there is room for huge winnings to be realized using credit to your advantage.

The winners know this, or have learned it through their own education. Perhaps their parents imparted the knowledge, or they read *Rich Dad/ Poor Dad*, *The Cash Flow Quadrant* and similar books. However the wisdom was arrived at, the formula can be very rewarding. First some obvious truths:

1. Banks make money by lending money. That's their business. We all know that.

2. Banks can lose money by making loans to people or projects that will never be paid back. Banks have to be careful. Some important lessons have been learned from the financial crisis starting in 2008. Like all of us, too many bad debts and there's trouble.

3. Banks like to make loans when they have security or collateral. If the loan isn't paid they want to latch onto something tangible and real to secure their repayment. Banks, like all of us, have to be careful in properly valuing their security interest.

Given these obvious truths, there is one additional obvious truth that rarely gets mentioned:

4. Banks do not make the lion's share of the money on certain loans. Credit winners who understand the system and use credit to their advantage make far more money (especially on certain real estate loans) than the banks will ever hope to make.

Appreciating this rarely discussed obvious truth can make you a lot of money too. Banks make their fair share lending money. You can make a far greater amount borrowing money for the right projects and for the right reasons.

You may be thinking at this moment that real estate and secured loans from banks are totally different from credit card offers.

Not true. A number of years ago my partner and I came across a quarter acre of raw land with highway frontage in Silver Springs, Nevada. The owner needed $5,000 quickly and there wasn't time to arrange for traditional bank financing. Credit cards came to the rescue. We knew we could each handle an extra $200 per month payment in order to pay off the loan in a reasonable time period. So we each took a $2,500 cash advance on our credit cards and bought the land.

In this case, the credit card company made a reasonable amount of money at their usual high interest rates and we have since paid off the principal amount. But the land was bought at the right price and we sold it for a handsome profit. We used our credit cards to make a lot more money than the credit card company did.

That's what credit winners do. And that's the purpose of this book. To get rid of negative credit habits, to clean up your credit and start positively using credit to your advantage.

But before you start winning with credit we've got your health to think about...

Chapter Three

Health Effects of Debt

Sick of Debt

Everyone in debt knows that debt can make you feel sick. You plan around it; you think about it; you worry about it. Many of us can trace our level of stress right back to our level of debt. A study at Ohio State University found that people who reported higher levels of stress in regard to their debt showed higher levels of physical impairment and reported worse health than their counterparts with lower levels of debt. The study also found that the level of credit card debt compared to income also played a role, with those with higher percentages of debt to income reporting a higher level of physical impairment.

Debt stress impacts physical and mental health as well as our relationships. The divorce rate is often said to be over 50 percent and the number one reason for divorce is reportedly financial trouble. Couples argue more about money than any other relationship issue.

Stress, anxiety and depression are common for those with uncomfortable amounts of debt. Feelings of guilt, shame and failure all impact self-esteem and lead people to feel as if they are out of control or powerless. Add to this the fears of what will happen if the bills are not paid, the aggressiveness of many creditors and debt collectors, and the constant pressure to continue spending, and it is no wonder that some Americans actually end up taking their own lives as a means to ending the downward spiraling feelings.

Debt stress has also been linked to substance abuse and the accompanying health problems (including an increased risk of violence) associated with this illegal activity. On the legal side, many people react to stress by abusing alcohol or legal prescriptions.

Spending has become such a problem for some people that the pharmaceutical industry has taken notice. Shopping has long been recognized as an addiction for those whose spending interferes significantly with their lives. In fact, it is estimated that 8 percent of American adults (90 percent of these being women) suffer from this addiction. Research has shown that this compulsive spending is linked to low serotonin levels in the brain. The drug Celexa increases serotonin and is now being used to treat compulsive shopping. In fact a recent study showed 80 percent of the shopping addicts treated with Celexa were able to curb their impulses to spend.

Another serious health concern related to financial problems is the fact that people will often forego treatment for physical (or mental) illness in attempts to control debt. This too often leads to more serious ailments and even death. In addition, those in financial turmoil are more likely to go against doctor's orders and return to work in order to pay the bills – medical bills included – thus increasing their chances of reinjury.

We all know about the connection between stress and illness. Get stressed and you get sick. Anyone who has ever gotten sick right after a big test or after the deadline for a huge project knows how stress wears us down. It's said that when the sex is good it only accounts for about 10 percent of the health of the marriage. When it's bad it accounts for about 90 percent. The same can be said for money and the stress it creates at work and at home. When the money is good, it accounts for only about 10 percent of a person's problems. But when it's bad it accounts for 90 percent.

Over the past decade, researchers have demonstrated the link between financial stress and health, as well as productivity in the workplace. For example, Financial Fitness reports that:

Distress over financial matters is contributing to irritability, anger, fatigue, and sleeplessness for over 52% of Americans. Among those who reported high stress levels due to debt, the following illnesses were reported:

- More than 3 times the ulcers or digestive tract problems (27% in the high stress group and 8% in the low stress group),

- 44% report trouble with migraines compared to 15% in the low stress group,

- 500% increase in severe anxiety and depression,

- Double the rate of heart attacks, and

- Increased sleep disturbances and lack of concentration.

They also cite a study published in *Diabetes Care* that found that "financial stress was shown to increase the risk of metabolic syndrome which can lead to serious medical conditions like diabetes, heart disease, high cholesterol, and obesity."

It doesn't take a researcher to tell most of us that when we're dealing with financial problems, we feel horrible.

Unfortunately, many people don't know where to turn when they have credit problems. This book is designed to help you understand your options so you can take control of your financial life.

Let's look at how a smart and resolute couple managed to do it...

Chapter Four

Beat the Lenders At Their Own Game

How We Got Out of Debt – Robert and Kim Kiyosaki's Story

While Robert and Kim enjoy tremendous financial success now, they too have experienced their share of tough times. This is their story, as told by Kim:

In 1985, Robert and I had a great deal of bad debt. And even though we kept making payments every month we never seemed to make a dent in the amount we owed. Each month we paid a little over the minimum on each one of our credit cards as well as on our car loan. Obviously there had to be a better way to get ourselves out from under our creditors. And sure enough there was.

This is the formula Robert and I followed to pay off our debt. You'll find that if you follow our formula you will be out of debt much quicker than you imagined. Most people find themselves "bad" debt-free within 5-7 years. The key is to stick with the formula. You will not get ahead if you say I'll just skip this month, and then two, and then three. If you stick with the formula it then becomes a habit you follow for a lifetime.

Here is the formula we used.

Step #1 – Stop accumulating bad debt. Whatever you purchase via credit cards must be paid off in full at the end of each month. No exceptions.

Step #2 – Make a list of all of your consumer (bad) debts. This includes each credit card, car loans, school loans, home improvement loans on your personal residence, and other bad debts you have acquired. (One item on my and Robert's list was an outstanding debt to a partner from one of Robert's past businesses). You can even include your home mortgage on this list.

Step #3 – Next to each item listed make three columns:

- Amount Owed
- Minimum monthly payment
- Number of months

Enter the appropriate numbers into each column. To arrive at the number of months, simply divide the amount owed by the minimum payment.

Step #4 – Based solely on the number of months, begin ranking each debt. Put a "1" next to the lowest number of months, a "2" next to the second-lowest number and continue up to the highest number of months. This is the order that you will be paying off your various debts.

The reason you start with the debt with the lowest number of months is that you want to have your first "win" or success in the program as soon as possible. Once you get that first credit card (or debt) paid off you'll begin to see the light at the end of the tunnel.

Step #5 – Come up with an additional $150-200 per month. If you are serious about getting out of debt, and more importantly becoming financially free, then generating this extra money will not be difficult. To be candid, if you cannot generate an additional $150 per month then your chances of becoming financially independent are slim. (You may need some of the resources in the next chapter to help you get back on track.)

Step #6 – Pay the minimum amount on every debt that you have listed except for the one you've marked with a "1". On this first debt to be paid off, pay the minimum amount due plus the additional $150-200. Keep doing this every month until your first debt is paid off. Scratch that debt from your list.

Step #7 – Congratulate yourself!

Step #8 – Pay the minimum amount due on every debt that you have listed except for the one you've marked with a "2". To this debt, pay the minimum amount due plus the entire amount you've been paying on debt #1. For example, on debt #1 your minimum amount due was $40, and you added the additional $150 so you were paying a total of $190 each month. On debt #2, if the minimum amount due is $50, you will now pay that $50 plus $190, for a total of $240 per month.

After each debt is paid off, take the total you were paying on that debt and add it to the minimum amount due on your next debt to get your new monthly payment. You will be amazed at how quickly this amount adds up and how quickly your credit cards, car loans, etc., are paid off.

Continue this process until all of the debts on your list are paid off.

Step #9 – Congratulate yourself.

Step #10 – By this time the monthly payment you were paying on your last debt is likely to be quite substantial. Keep paying that amount every month. Except now, instead of paying it to your creditors, you can pay it to yourself until you build an emergency savings fund and then start investing. You're on your way to building wealth!

The method Robert and Kim described is very powerful. In fact you may be able to slash the amount of time and money it takes to pay off your debt dramatically. For example, let's say you have the following debts:

Lender	APR	Current Balance	Monthly Payment
VISA	15.9%	$4,150	$58
MasterCard	12.9%	$3,645	$73
Retail card	18.9%	$4,595	$115
Installment Loan	17.5%	$1,990	$50
Total		$14,380	$296

Guess how long it will take you to pay off that $14,380 debt if you are making the minimum payments?

Only 182 years and one month.

And you'll pay over $72,000 in interest. In Biblical times the lender would be stoned to death for such usury.

How can those numbers possibly be so high? In a nutshell, it's due to tiny minimum payments that go down as your balance goes down. Unlike a car loan where you'll have a fixed payment that will pay off your loan in, say, four or five years, credit card issuers figure your monthly payments as a percentage of the amount you owe. The minimum payment is already small, which is great when you need to make a small payment, but lousy when you can't pay more. As you pay down the balance, the monthly payment goes down and the debt gets s-t-r-e-t-c-h-e-d out.

The debt reduction strategy that Robert and Kim used has several powerful elements, and I've added one more tip to the mix to help make you successful even faster. Here's why it works:

1. **You keep your total monthly payment fixed**. This is the first way to beat the card issuers at their own game. In our example, the total monthly payment is $296. As you pay down your debts, the amount your credit card issues will require you to pay will become smaller. But you won't fall for it. You'll pay at least $296 each month until all the debts are paid. Just doing that alone cuts the repayment period from 182 years and 1 month down to just under 15 years and saves you over $63,000 in interest. You can put down that Biblical rock.

2. **You stop charging**. If you must have a card for business purposes only, keep it out of the plan. Let your business promptly pay off that card. But for personal purchases don't use a credit card. You've heard the saying: If you're in a hole, stop digging.

3. **You add extra if you can**. If you can afford an extra $50 a month on our example, you'll be debt-free in just five years you'll save over $65,000 in interest. Whew!

4. **You target only one debt at a time**. If you try to do too many things at once you'll lose focus and won't get anywhere. If you focus on paying one debt off at a time, you'll be much more successful. For maximum savings, you should target the highest rate debt first. However, if you're like Kim and Robert and want to see some fast results, focus on the lowest balance first.

5. **You'll have a plan**. Research by the Consumer Federation of America and the Bank of America found that people with as little as $10,000 a year in income who reported having a written plan had twice as much money in savings and investments as those without a plan. The same principle applies when you are getting out of debt. Having a written plan can give you that discipline and motivation you need.

Here are several different strategies for reducing debt as illustrated by the Debt Reduction Report below:

Debt Reduction Report

Complete Debt Summary	
Number of Debts	4
Start Month	April 2010
Payment Plan	Immediate
Payoff Strategy	APR
Balance Owed	$14,380
Monthly Payments	$296
Pledge Money	$50
Payments + Pledge	$346

Minimum Payment from Statement	
Debt-Free Date	April 2192
Months Required	2185
Total Interest Paid	$72,333
Total Money Paid	$86,713

Minimum Payment Held Constant	
Debt-Free Date	December 2028
Months Required	225
Total Interest Paid	$14,209
Total Money Paid	$28,589
Money Saved	**$58,124**
Time Saved	**163 years 4 months**

Debt Blaster without Pledge Money	
Debt-Free Date	November 2016
Months Required	80
Total Interest Paid	$9,169
Total Money Paid	$23,549
Money Saved	**$63,164**

Debt Blaster with Pledge Money	
Debt-Free Date	April 2015
Months Required	61
Total Interest Paid	$6,645
Total Money Paid	$21,025
Money Saved	**$65,688**

Time Saved   175 years 5 months   Time Saved   177 years 0 months

Debt Blaster™ Copyright 1991-2012 by Michael J. Riley. See Resources section.

Here's a brief explanation of the various repayment strategies described in the Debt Reduction Report:

- **Minimum Payment from Statement:** This example shows how much you would pay, and how long it would take to get out of debt, if you made only the issuer's required minimum payments each month. As explained above, your minimum required payments decline as your balance goes down, stretching out the debt for a long time.

- **Minimum Payment Held Constant:** Here's how long it would take to pay off your debt if you continued making the minimum payments currently required by your statement. This corresponds with Robert and Kim Kiyosaki's instructions about dividing the balance by the current minimum payment. It's faster than paying the declining minimum payments and will save you money in the long run.

- **Debt Blaster without Pledge Money:** This describes how long it would take you to pay off the debt if you turbocharge your payment plan as we described. You stick with the same total monthly payment that you must make now, but as you pay down some debts you put the "extra" amount above the minimum payment toward the highest rate debt until it's paid off, and so on.

- **Debt Blaster with Pledge Money:** If you can add some extra money toward your total monthly payment you'll get out of debt faster. In this example, we added just $50 per month but saved much more than that in interest.

What you're doing here is creating a tsunami effect. It will seem very slow at first, but as soon as you start paying off a debt or two your plan will pick up speed and you'll start seeing dramatic effects.

If you've ever had a mortgage you probably noticed that in the first several years most of your payment went towards interest, not principal (principal is the amount you borrowed). But several years into the loan it starts shifting and near the end your payment is mostly principal, not interest. Why does most of the interest get paid off first? Because so many people refinance long before the loan is paid off. Nowadays lenders want to earn as much interest as possible in the loan's early years. They don't make money when you pay off principal, so the principal payments are very low at the start and only grow once most of the interest (read, profit) has been paid off.

Turbocharge Your Debt-Free Plan

The lower your interest rate, the faster you'll get out of debt. Many people are still trapped in high-rate credit card debt, at interest rates ranging from 19.98% to 29.99% or even higher.

You'll turbo charge your plan if you also try to get the lowest rates possible. As you start to pay off your credit cards, you should constantly be looking for ways to lower your interest rates.

Talk Your Way Out of Debt

Scott Bilker is the author of *Talk Your Way Out of Credit Card Debt*. His website is found at debtsmart.com. Scott has made and recorded hundreds of calls with banks in his efforts to lower interest rates for himself, family and friends. In his book, he uses this real-life illustration:

He made 52 phone calls that took 403 minutes (6 hours, 43 minutes) and saved $43,147.68. That's an average savings of $107.07 per minute. Wouldn't you like to save over a hundred bucks a minute? Even $100 per hour is good.

Scott has over 50 credit cards and he has paid 0% interest on his balances for the past 15 years. He also has maintained a great credit score, and routinely racks up all kinds of rewards. He's clearly a credit winner.

Here is an excerpt from an interview where Gerri Detweiler, our contributing editor and the host of Talk Credit Radio, asked Scott about his strategies for getting lower credit card rates:

Gerri: Scott, you know, I think there's a sense these days that sometimes people feel lucky they even have a credit card and have a credit line. So really, what are issuers willing to do now in terms of negotiating with customers?

Scott: *Well, you know, it's still true that banks need profitable customers to be profitable. So as consumers, we do hold the cards so to speak because we decide where we spend out money. And even if interest rates aren't the best for banks, they still make money by charging merchant's fees.*

Gerri: There are a lot people that are still paying pretty hefty interest rates, given the fact that these banks are paying practically nothing to borrow this money.

Scott: *Yeah, that's absolutely true. It's not like the banks are going to lower the interest rates just because they're getting a better deal. The only time banks are going to give out really good rates are to credit cardholders who have excellent credit scores and have had a relationship with the bank for years.*

Gerri: For a long time, there was no downside to asking for a lower rate. Then we went through a period about I'd say, 2009, when it actually got a little bit risky because sometimes it would trigger an account review and (your issuer) would say, "Oh gee, well you have a lot of credit card debt, we'd like to lower your credit limit," and that lowers your score and when your score goes down your other (credit lines may) get lowered. So tell me, where we are and where have we been in this process?

Scott: *Well you're absolutely right, it might've been a little riskier before but if you're paying high rates and if you're getting gouged for a lot of fees, it's important to stop that. So it's always important to call the banks and try to negotiate better rates and have fees waived. Today, you know, the swing is now towards more credit card usage in the last few months. There had been many reports that people are now using their credit cards more, certainly during this holiday season. So once again, the banks have to decide if they're going to give good deals to people or if they're going to let people just transfer the balances or use (other) cards during the season.*

Gerri: Let's talk about what you do if you feel that your credit card rate is too high. What do you think is too high these days?

Scott: *You know, anything you're paying is too high.*

Gerri: Really?

Scott: *Unless it's zero. Just look at your credit card statement right now, whatever it is, if it's not zero you want to try to get towards zero, I mean, zero is perfect. I gotta tell you, I haven't paid any interests for like, 15 years already. I mean zero, absolutely nothing.*

Gerri: Tell me what your credit score is. It has to be pretty good.

Scott: *It's 790. It's been better. Yesterday it was 790, but the best it's ever been is 819.*

Gerri: That's out of 850 on a FICO score, so that's still a prime credit score.

Scott: *Yeah, it's a good score. Anything over 720 is quite good and you know, I've got 50 credit cards.*

Gerri: You still have 50?

Scott: *Yes. I used to have like 60 but a whole bunch of them got lost during that credit crunch.*

Gerri: Okay, I want to talk about that a little bit later on the show. But let's start with what to do when you talk to your credit card companies. So we've talked about the fact that you do want to negotiate if you're paying more than 0%. You get on the phone, you're a little bit nervous, what do you say to them?

Scott: *That's exactly why I wrote my book. Just for a moment about the book because it's important: The reason why I did this is for that very reason. People are nervous, they don't know what to say so what I did was I recorded the banks. You know, how when you call the banks they record us for training purposes? Well I recorded them for training purposes, to train everyone on how to deal with the banks. So the book has a whole bunch of calls - the actual transcripts from the calls.*

Gerri: And that's your book - Talk Your Way Out of Credit Card Debt, right?

Scott: *Yes, so that way people can read through them and kind of get a feel for what's going to happen.*

Gerri: Let me add just real quick, you've made a lot these calls, right?

Scott: *Yes, in the book I have 52 but I've made hundreds. I just picked the ones that would represent the basic outcome that you would have. So I would say that, you know, if you're nervous about calling there are many things you can do but you should always call. There's nothing to be nervous about. Just pick up the phone, give them a call and the very first person, let's say for example we're going to, let's say, do something* *easy like waive a late fee. That's pretty easy to do. If you have a late fee and you're listening right now, after we're done, call your bank, get that thing waived especially if it's your first one. Just call up, talk to the first person - hey, I was looking at my credit card statement, I noticed this late fee, can you waive that fee for me? And I have never heard of a case for a first-time late fee when they didn't waive the fee. They always waive that fee no matter what, throughout the years, they always do it.*

Gerri: So you don't have to have some kind of good excuse as to why you were late? You just have to ask for them to waive it?

Scott: *Yep, that's correct. And you can make up an excuse if you want but it doesn't matter, they're going to waive it. I've never heard of somebody calling for the first time and not having it waived. And I've made dozens and dozens of calls just for that thing, just for that purpose - having the first late fee waived. Even if you've had a couple late fees in a row they'll still waive one or two of them. They might not waive them all, if you have say 6 in a row it's going to be a little trickier, you know, you might have to call and let them know they're going to get paid. But the bottom line is, if you do something like that, just call up, talk to the first person they'll probably be able to do it. Now when you try to lower interest rates or do more difficult things like multiple late fees, something like that, chances are the very first person you're going to speak to will not be able to do it. So you're going to ask to speak to their supervisor, say, "Hey can I talk to your supervisor?" They're going to say, probably, my supervisor's going to tell you the same thing. And you just say, "Wonderful, I want to talk to your supervisor anyway." Then the supervisor's going to get on the phone, you're going to go through the whole thing again and now we'll see what the supervisor's going to do. If you're just asking, it's going to be difficult. You say things like, well, you want to have a deal breaker ready, something you're going to do when they don't do what you want. So you say, "Listen, I got all these credit offers, I want to transfer my balance so what do you want to do? Do you want to just lower my rate or get rid of this fee or am I just going to leave you and not do business with you and close my account?"*

Now prior to, say 2009 that you were saying, that worked really well. After that, I definitely heard of cases where people would say they didn't care, they said okay, close my account. And I even had that experience too before my business cards during this time period. They said I didn't use the card but I just bought an airline ticket the month before, it's like a thousand dollars! They're like, well, you didn't use it before that. I'm like, are you kidding me? They're actually closing my account because of it - because of inactivity. I just spent a thousand dollars last month and over the last 10 years I spent almost $25,000!

Gerri: Okay, so if your issuer says no, you talk to a supervisor then at that point do you give up on that issuer?

Scott: *Well, that might be. You know, and if you go through the whole thing, I'm going to close my account and you're persistent. What I like to do too is I'll run the numbers because I use Quicken. I'll just tell them how much I spent, like in that case with the business card. I'll be like, well I spent $10,000 over the last 5 years and this much of it was interest, of course in my case it's zero so all they're getting is the merchant fees. But they're getting merchant fees on that and interest, and I'm like, you really want to let that go? And again, they're not too bright so sometimes they'll be like "sure." But if that's the problem, if that happens you have many options. At Credit.com there are a whole bunch of credit cards you can turn to get lower rates and I would start there and start looking for a new bank if you don't have one. But if you do, the best place to turn to transfer your balance when banks don't do what you want are to the other credit cards that you have, that you've had for awhile. Like I've said, I have 50 cards, people think it's ridiculous, you know. If I use them all Gerri, today's show would be about bankruptcy and how to get out of it, because I cannot use all those cards and pay them all. So what happens is I have so many cards with a zero balance that if anyone of the few cards that I'm using gives me trouble and then they don't do what I want when I want call up to try to negotiate better rates and better deals, then I'll just call all the other ones - and its the same kind of negotiation. I want to now shop for* *another rate but I've got a lot of calls I can make. So I'll call one bank, "Hey I want to transfer my balance to you, I'll transfer $10,000 right now but you got to give me zero or 1% or whatever's better than what I'm getting now." And I'll just go through all of them until someone does that, but I have a lot of options. That's why I like to have a lot of open lines of credit.*

In the interview Scott goes on to explain how he takes advantage of credit card rewards programs. For example, in addition to not paying interest for years, he hasn't paid for a movie ticket in years - and he has three kids. As he says, "That's a lot of popcorn and movie tickets." Listen to Gerri's interview with Scott at GerriDetweiler.com

As Scott points out, if you want your card company to lower your interest rate, you have to ask. They may or may not, but you won't know unless you try. As my father (and yours too, probably) always said: "It never hurts to ask." So, go ahead, stand tall and ask for a rate reduction.

The main reason card issuers will often negotiate with you is because they want to keep cardholders with balances. After all, that's how they make money. Many times they'd rather lower your interest rate than lose you as a customer. Of course this means you're not going to call and threaten to pay off your entire balance unless they lower your rate. What incentive does the issuer have there? None. So state that you're better able to make the monthly payments with a lower rate. That's what they want to hear. Then, when you get the lower rate, work to pay the entire balance off.

Many people are intimidated by the thought of negotiating with their credit card company. There is no need to feel this way. Just remember the other thing my father always said: "He who cares least, wins."

You can be sure that the credit card company really doesn't care about you as an individual, or about your unique concerns and issues. You are a billing unit, one of millions of indistinguishable billing units. You exist merely to provide profit. And let's be honest, if you ran the company you'd see it that way too.

But if they care that little about you (and they do care – that little), why then should you care what they think about you?

Be assured that the customer service representative you speak with won't remember you an hour later. They speak with hundreds and hundreds of people every day. Do you really think that they go home at night and gossip about the embarrassing credit problems John in Des Moines is experiencing? Don't flatter yourself. The fact is, your customer service representative these days probably lives in India and goes home at night worrying about his or her own financial problems, not yours. They may be worried about putting food on their own table. How do you rate on their continuum? Food on the table ... John in Des Moines. Your insignificant problems don't even register in their consciousness.

Now that we have the context established, stop caring what these understandably uncaring people think about you and start negotiating to your advantage. Ask for lower rates and do it without a care. They're not going to bite you or write you down for asking. They don't care. And neither do you. And by caring least about it, not worrying about it, not having one cautious doubt about it, you will win.

Another way to win is to simply transfer balance to cheaper cards. If you still have plenty of credit available, this can be a terrific money saver. Call each of your issuers and tell them you have credit card balances, and are shopping for the lowest rate to consolidate those balances. Ask them what they can do for you. (It's helpful to keep notes on what each one offers). If you're not up to your eyeballs in debt, or have poor credit, you should get some very good offers.

Look out for the following when you're doing this:

- Balance transfer fees can add up. Some issuers will charge a transfer fee of as much as 2-4% of the transfer amount. In the past, these fees were often capped at $50 - $75 but now they are often unlimited. Ask about this fee and try to get it waived if it's high.

- Tiered rates. If you already have a $2000 balance on a card at, say, 18%, and you transfer a new balance of, say, $1000 at 4.9%, issuers traditionally will apply your payments to paying down the 4.9% part of the balance first. This is the exact opposite of what I recommend if you're trying to get out of debt. Thanks to the Credit CARD Act, however, there is a way to pay off that higher rate balance without having to first eliminate the low-rate balance. Here's the trick: Under the CARD Act, any payment you make above the minimum payment must be applied to the higher rate portion of your balance. So try to pay as much as you can above the minimum to reduce that higher rate portion of your balance as quickly as possible.

- If your card issuers won't budge, you may have to play hardball with them, or get a professional to help you. We'll explain how to do that later in this book.

But first, let's review consolidating...

Chapter Five

Debt Consolidation

Should I Get A Consolidation Loan?

The ideal scenario for someone with debt is to get a low-rate consolidation loan and pay it off in three or four years. But that's easier said than done. True consolidation loans are usually unsecured personal loans (we'll talk about other types of consolidation loans in a moment). The problem is that lenders know that if you already have quite a bit of debt and then consolidate, you're likely to end up deeper in debt in a year or two.

Remember our five types of borrowers:

> Wishers
> Wasters
> Wanters
> Whiners
> Winners

Wishers, wasters, wanters, and whiners are all at risk when it comes to consolidation loans. They will often:

- Get a consolidation loan based solely on the monthly payment. Once they've consolidated, they figure they'll be able to quickly pay it off but have no specific plan for doing so.

- Soon run up new debt. After all they still need a new car, clothing, the latest cell phone, etc.

- Be at risk for high-rate consolidation loans because they are focused just on today's situation and not on a big picture plan for getting out of debt.

- Complain about their situation but never try to take steps to remedy it.

- For winners, though, a consolidation loan is just a way to lower costs in order to get out of debt faster. They'll take a consolidation loan if it makes sense, but they won't fall for gimmicks like high-rate loans.

Lenders know that there are a lot of wishers, wanters, wasters and whiners out there. That's how they make money. They also know that puts their loans at risk, especially since they don't have any collateral to go after if you don't pay.

That makes a consolidation loan hard to get if you already have quite a bit of credit card debt. You can shop for a consolidation loan, but what you're more like to find are offers to tap the equity in your home (where lenders at least can foreclose if they really have to), offers for credit counseling and debt settlement (which we'll talk about in the next chapter).

Peer to Peer (P2P) Loans

If your credit card company is charging you a high rate and won't budge, you may want to check out a peer to peer lending service (also called "social lending" service). Although the premise is similar to that of a bank (take in money and then lend out that money at a higher rate), these services aren't banks. Instead, they allow individuals to lend money to other individuals in the hopes of earning higher returns on their investments. The two most popular services in this space are Prosper.com and LendingClub.com.

You don't have to have perfect credit to get a P2P loan, but you typically must have a decent credit score. Their minimum credit score requirements are posted on their websites. The interest rate you will pay will depend on the level of risk the lenders think they are taking by lending you money. The better your credit qualifications, the lower the rate you'll pay.

In addition to potentially lower interest rates and (possibly) easier credit standards, there's another advantage to these loans over credit cards. These loans must be paid back over a specific number of months, so you won't be stretching out the debt over many years. And they will be reported as installment loans, not revolving loans, which may also be helpful for your credit scores.

Home Loans for Debt Consolidation

Home equity loans were one of the most popular ways to consolidate over the last decade. Unfortunately, as real estate values dropped, many homeowners found themselves upside down on their homes, and owing more than their homes were worth. If you didn't take money out during the boom and you now find yourself with equity in your home, consider yourself fortunate. Still, if your personal finances have taken a hit during the recession you may be tempted to tap your home equity to pay off other debt. There are two basic ways to do this:

- Get a home equity loan or line of credit
- Refinance your current loan and get "cash out" to pay off debt

There's always a risk – and it's a real one – that you could lose your home if you can't pay a home equity loan or the new mortgage. Recently, we've seen foreclosures at an all-time high. With credit card debt, the worst that will happen if you run into tough times is that the account will be charged off and sent to collections. Eventually you may be sued. But, unlike the home equity or mortgage loans, you can't immediately lose your home just because you don't pay your credit card bill.

Home equity loans can be deceptive, since it makes it appear that you are turning bad debt into good debt. But when you trade credit card debt for home equity debt, you're giving up the opportunity to take that home equity and turn it into good debt – perhaps by leveraging it to buy investment property. Instead you're just sucking out your equity to pay for expenses and high interest rates you may have incurred long ago. Unfortunately, many people consolidate using their home and then they end up with new credit card debts a year or two later – only now their home is maxxed out. Unless things are truly on the upswing for you financially, it's probably wise to avoid putting your home at risk.

Home Equity Loans

These loans come in two flavors: The first are home equity loans which are for a fixed amount with a fixed repayment period. The second are home equity lines of credit which are more like a credit card, allowing you to borrow up to a certain amount and pay it back with more flexibility.

Many home equity plans set a fixed period during which you can borrow money. At the end of this "draw" period (which might be ten years, for example), you will not be able to borrow any more. You may have to pay the balance due then, or you may have another period (ten years, for example) during which you must repay the loan. Some plans may require you to take out a minimum amount when you first get the loan or may impose a prepayment penalty if you pay off the loan in the first or second year.

The great thing about home equity loans is that they usually carry low interest rates, the interest you do pay is often tax-deductible if you itemize, and the payments are relatively low. Many home equity lines, for example, allow you to pay only interest each month.

They are also relatively easy to get if you have OK credit and enough equity in your home. And, best of all, they usually carry low – or even no – closing costs. You may have to pay for an appraisal, but often you don't have to pay for much more than that.

Warning! If you are currently paying on a home equity loan, you may be making interest-only payments. Your monthly payments can rise dramatically when you enter the full payback period. Be sure to check with your lender to find out when that will happen and plan accordingly.

Refinancing

Another way to tap the equity in your home is to refinance. This is especially attractive if your current mortgage has a high interest rate or if you want to start over again with a new, longer mortgage.

A "cash out" refinance allows you to refinance your mortgage, pay off the current loan, and take additional cash out to pay off debts. You may be able to borrow up to 80% of the value of your home in a cash-out refinance, but that depends on your credit score and whether you are self-employed. (Lower credit scores and self-employment may mean you can't borrow quite as much on a cash-out transaction.)

Why would you want to get a longer mortgage? Simple: If your monthly payments come down for your house, you will have more money each month to pay down your other obligations. Don't be one of the millions who refinanced before the Great Recession only to use the money on doodads and non-performing assets, and eventually lost their house when values fell. If you refinance, keep paying down your other debt with any money you free up each month by refinancing.

Refinancing isn't usually free. Closing costs usually add up to about 4% of the mortgage amount. Some lenders offer no-cost refinancing, but you'll pay a higher interest rate. Analyze the loan and the numbers involved to make sure it is the right step for you.

Retirement Loans for Debt Consolidation

Edgar had several credit cards totaling about $35,000 in balances. One issuer in particular had raised his rate to 29.99% and wouldn't budge. That really bugged him, so Edgar decided he'd cash in his IRA and use the funds to pay off that debt. However, that was an expensive choice. Since he had taken a tax deduction when he'd contributed to his IRA, the money he took out was subject to taxes as income, plus he had to pay a 10% penalty for early withdrawal. That made Edgar's strategy a costly one.

Borrowing against your retirement plan may be a better option than taking an early withdrawal. You may be able to borrow against your 401(k), 403(b) or pension account, but not against your IRA.

Most plans allow you to borrow up to 50% of the value of your account and pay it back over five years. Interest is charged, but it's usually a fairly low rate and you pay it to yourself, not to a lender. Another benefit is that you don't have to have good credit to borrow, since there is no credit check. Of course there are drawbacks. The big risk if you take one of these loans through your employer-sponsored plan and then leave (or lose) your job, you may have to pay back the loan immediately or pay the taxes and penalties as if it were an early withdrawal. Ouch!

Here's another big risk: The chance that it won't solve your problem and you'll end up in bankruptcy anyway. Let's say you've gotten yourself into a lot of debt because of pay cuts at work or a business that went under. So you start raiding your retirement funds. It takes you longer to get back on your feet than you expected. You are unable to pay back the retirement loan, so you are forced to treat the loan as a withdrawal and pay taxes and a 10% penalty. You still end up in bankruptcy. Now your retirement funds, which likely would have been protected in bankruptcy, are gone. You're literally starting from scratch.

Friends and Family

Friends or family may be willing to help you out if you're in a rough spot. But please think twice before asking them to do that. Are you really sure that you can pay back the loan? Really, really sure? If not, you're just dragging them into your financial problems.

Your parents, richer older brother or any other friend or relative do not "owe" you anything, even if they make gobs more money than you do. Allowing them to bail you out may temporarily help the situation but unless your problems are truly out of the ordinary for you, the relief won't last. That's because you need to learn how to stop taking on bad debt and build wealth.

If you – or they – are determined to make one of these loans, then at least make it professional. Get an official promissory note and set up an official repayment schedule. And treat it as any other loan, not as a gift. Visit the Resource section for more information.

Prepaying Your Mortgage

For some people a mortgage is considered "good debt." That's because you're largely using the bank's money to purchase an asset that likely will increase over time. It's called "leverage."

While paying off your credit cards and other bad debt should be your first priority, there are times when it can make sense to pay off your mortgage faster than the 30-year or 15-year loan you've taken out.

Advantages of Prepaying

- You'll keep more money in your pocket. A typical home loan costs 2 – 3 times the original loan amount in interest. That's money will be yours, instead of your banker's, if you prepay.
- You'll own your home free and clear sooner. For many people, that gives them a tremendous amount of comfort. (Be sure to protect all that equity you have with a homestead exemption or other asset protection strategy.)
- Building up equity may give you more flexibility if you need to move, or even borrow against your home for other investments or a business. A highly leveraged house can quickly become a burden if times get tough.

Disadvantage of Prepaying

- When interest rates are low on home loans, you don't get a huge bang for your buck by prepaying. (Although you may still "earn" the equivalent of a return greater than the paltry amount paid on savings accounts.)

- You may lose some of the tax advantages of deductible mortgage interest. Keep in mind, though, that if your interest costs and other itemized expenses don't exceed the standard deduction, you're not getting a deduction anyway.

- Home equity is not very liquid. It's easy to borrow against when your financial situation is fine, but if you run into problems and you may have trouble qualifying for a loan. (That's why it's good to line up a home equity loan before you really need it.)

Here's the bottom line: Pay off your bad debt first. Then make sure you have an adequate emergency savings fund, plus good insurance (health, life, auto and an umbrella policy). Then if you have extra money you'd like to use to prepay your mortgage, go ahead. Don't forget to keep focusing on wealth-building rather than just debt reduction as your end goal. If prepaying your mortgage fits into that plan by all means do it.

How to Win at Debt Consolidation

Have you noticed one thing about the options we've described in this chapter? They may all help you to lower your cost and/or your payments as you get out of debt, but you still must find the income to pay them off.

There are several ways to do this:

- **Cut expenses.** Start tracking where you spend your money and look for ways to cut back. It may not be fun, but think of it as temporary. One of the best ways to do this is to start paying attention to what you're spending and see if you can find ways to cut even a little. Every extra dollar you free up can help you cut your debt faster. I've included a Budget Worksheet in the Appendix to help you learn where your money is going.

- **Bring in more income.** One of the best ways to do this may be to have your own business. This may save you money in taxes and bring in extra cash, as well as other benefits.

But for now, let's get some more help...

Chapter Six

Getting Help

Sometimes you need more than just a payment schedule to get out of debt. If you're constantly juggling payments, robbing Peter to pay Paul, or using the credit cards to fill in the gaps in your budget, more help may be in order. Here are your options when your debt is getting to be too much.

As you consider these options, keep in mind that wishers are going to skim over them, hoping that someone – or something (the raise, the big investment) is going to come along and keep them from having to really deal with their debt. Wasters are going to avoid these options because they may temporarily cut off their spending lifeline – their credit cards; wanters will think these methods will take too long and require too much effort ; while whiners are just going to focus on all the possible downsides (especially damage to their credit ratings). Winners are going to carefully evaluate these options as a potential tool to help them get to their ultimate goal; to be free of expensive consumer debt so they can start building wealth.

Credit Counseling

You've no doubt seen the ads for companies promising to "consolidate your debt." Often these ads are for credit counseling agencies. These agencies have been around for many years, and were created to help debtors find an alternative to bankruptcy. Here's what happens when you enter one of these programs:

They will collect information about your debts and finances. If it looks like you have the ability to pay off your debt in three to five years, they will fill out a proposal for each of your creditors and request that you be allowed to participate in a payment program at reduced interest rates and/or fees in most cases. (There are a few creditors who won't participate, or who won't offer more attractive terms.) If all goes well, you'll be offered a Debt Management Plan (DMP) to get you out of debt in 3 to 5 years in most cases.

When you enter a counseling program, you'll typically make one monthly payment to the agency which then pays all your participating creditors. It's not true consolidation in the sense that you're still on the hook for all the original debts. If the agency doesn't make your payments, guess who's still responsible?

In addition, some types of debts can't be included, such as student loans, tax debts, mortgages, car loans, etc. The agency may have other programs to help you with those debts but they typically can't be included in a DMP.

There are hundreds of counseling agencies across the country. Some lenders work with nearly a thousand agencies. What that means for you is that you shouldn't expect each of your individual payment plans will be "negotiated" with your lenders. Instead, the lender will have policies about what it offers for consumers in counseling. Some major card issuers, for example, will drop the interest rate to zero for consumers in counseling, while others won't drop it at all. It depends on each creditor.

Typically, you end up paying anywhere from 1.2 to 1.5 times your original debt by the time you complete the program. So if you start the program owing $10,000, you'll probably pay between $12,000 and $15,000 by the time the program is done. That may be a bargain compared to the amount you would have paid if you hadn't gone this route and just continued to make minimum payments. Again, it depends on what interest rates you'll pay on each of your debts and how long it takes you to complete your program.

When credit counseling doesn't work for consumers, it's for a variety of reasons.

As credit expert Gerri Detweiler has found in her research and writing, some consumers aren't realistic about their debt situation. They sign up for a counseling program agreeing to a monthly payment that gives them very little budget breathing room. Then a couple of emergencies crop up and they can't keep up with the program. Remember, it usually takes three to five years to complete a counseling program. While you're in the program you generally won't have access to new credit, which is what you probably relied up on in the past for emergencies.

Another potential problem is consumers may get sucked in by a counseling agency that charges high fees or doesn't make the payments to creditors on time. When either happens you may find yourself deeper in debt. This doesn't happen as much as it did several years ago, but you still want to make sure you are dealing with a reputable agency.

How does counseling affect your credit reports?

This is likely the #1 question many consumers ask about going into credit counseling. If you've been paying your bills on time, you may be worried that your good credit will quickly become bad credit. Here are some things you should understand:

1. Even if you pay every bill on time, your credit may not be as stellar as you think.

    A study by Experian Consumer Direct℠ found that:
    * More than 16 percent of the U.S. population use at least 50 percent of their available credit
    * The national average credit score for those with credit card utilization of at least 50 percent is 631 compared to the overall national average of 678

    You'll learn more about how credit scores work in the second half of this book, but suffice to say that if you've maxxed out your credit cards, your credit score is hurting as a result. Reducing your debt can help improve your credit. And once you're debt-free it will likely be a lot easier to rebuild your credit than you imagined.

2. The popular FICO scores don't specifically count against you for being in credit counseling when calculating your score (again, you'll learn more about FICO scores later in this book).

3. Most creditors will "re-age" your account once you've made three successful on-time payments through the counseling agency. That means they will delete late payments reported immediately before you enter the program.

Counseling agencies came under fire a decade ago for charging excessive fees, abusing their non-profit status by funneling money to for-profit affiliates, and for misleading consumers about their programs. In fact, in 2003 the FTC sued one of the largest counseling agencies for just those reasons, and in 2004 the US Senate held hearings on abusive counseling agencies. They found some of the agencies were abusing both their tax exempt status, as well as consumer trust.

Since then, most of the bad guys had their tax-exempt status revoked, went out of business, or both. And despite all that bad publicity, keep in mind that not all counseling agencies are bad! In fact, many have quietly been doing a lot of good work for many years. A good counseling agency may be able to help you avoid bankruptcy and further problems. But you will want to choose one very carefully. Visit the Resource section for information about how to find a reputable agency.

Debt Settlement

As the economy spiraled downward, millions of people found themselves unable to pay their bills. Debt settlement agencies saw this as an opportunity and began aggressively marketing debt relief solutions to consumers. The most common promise? Pay off your debt for pennies on the dollars and avoid bankruptcy. Step right up...

Debt settlement can be a legitimate option for someone struggling with a lot of credit card debt. It can be especially helpful for business owners, and those who own property (such as real estate) that they don't want to lose in bankruptcy. But it's also crucial you understand what it can and cannot do.

Here's what it involves:

You stop making your payments to your unsecured creditors. Instead you start making a regular monthly payment to a savings account. (These payments are typically lower than the minimum payments you probably have been making, but the more you save, the sooner you'll be able to put your debts behind you.) After your debts go unpaid for a few months, your lenders will likely call and/or write with offers to help you bring your accounts up-to-date. In some cases, they may offer a hardship program that will lower the interest rate – sometimes to 0% for a year. If you don't bite, you may be offered a settlement deal: Pay $x amount and your balance will be considered paid in full. If you aren't able to come to an agreement, your debt will typically be charged off by the lender. (This usually happens when you haven't made a payment in 6 months.) When a debt is charged off, it means the lender writes it off the as a bad debt. It does not mean the lender can't still try to collect.

While all this is happening, you are building up your savings account. At any time before or after charge-off, you or the debt negotiation firm you've hired can negotiate settlements on your debts. Sometimes settlements are as low as 10 - 25 cents on the dollar, but more often they are in the 50% range. Creditors are not required to settle debts.

Under most programs, you will be completely out of debt (at least unsecured debt) in anywhere from 12 – 36 months depending on your total debt and the money you are able to save to settle. When all is said and done you're your total payoff should be around 50 – 60% of the amount of debt that you entered the program with, including the fees charged by the settlement company (if you used one).

So if you have $20,000 in debt, you might enter a debt settlement program with a monthly payment for two years of $500, and settle your debts for a total of $12,000 including fees. Obviously, the final numbers will depend on your individual situation.

In late 2010, the Federal Trade Commission announced new rules for-profit debt settlement and credit counseling agencies must follow. They developed these rules in response to the numerous complaints lodged against firms that charged high upfront fees but did nothing to help those clients get out of debt.

Under the new rules, settlement firms:

- May not charge upfront fees. Fees may not be charged until debt is settled. You are entitled to a disclosure of the estimated fees.

- Must ensure that the money clients save in a dedicated savings account is under the consumer's control and out of the control of the settlement firm. You must be able to withdraw your money at any time without penalty.

- Must provide specific disclosures to clients, including the fact that settlement can negatively impact one's credit rating, and that taxes may be due on forgiven debt.

One of the most common fears people face when considering debt settlement is the fear that they are somehow immorally wiggling out of debts they legitimately owe. Don't be so harsh on yourself.

First of all, there is nothing immoral about paying back as much as you can. Life happens and people run into problems. The credit card companies know that when they extend huge credit lines and hike up interest rates to 25% plus, some people won't be able to pay them back. They are still enormously profitable.

Secondly, if you are in a hardship situation and don't take this step then your next option will likely be bankruptcy. In that case, your creditors may get nothing.

So do what you have to do. Pay what you can. Then get on with your life so you can focus on building wealth, which benefits our entire economy (including the credit card companies).

Another question to ask is whether you can settle your debts by yourself or whether you need to hire a company to help you. The card companies say that consumers should never hire debt negotiation firms, but that's not surprising. It's a lot easier to intimidate a cardholder who doesn't have any experience negotiating with creditors into paying as much as possible, than it would be if that person had the knowledge and expertise of a reputable settlement agency behind him or her.

Although many credit card companies won't admit it publicly, all of them negotiate settlements through these firms every day. If you are timid, overwhelmed, or just too busy to effectively negotiate with all of your creditors, it can be helpful to get professional advice. There are firms that coach consumers through the process if they want to do it themselves, as well as full-service firms that handle as much of the negotiations as possible for clients. The right choice depends on your time, energy and confidence that you can get the best deal possible.

Settling Debt

Rick's dream was to open a restaurant and at the age of 27, he turned it into a reality. His good sense of timing and taste made it an instant success. For a couple of years he lived the high life – plenty of money, local prestige and what seemed like a very bright future.

At the restaurant, Rick met his future wife. Within six months they were married. In another six months they were expecting their first child.

In the meantime, business was slowing down. Construction along the road where his restaurant was located made it difficult to park, so many patrons stayed away. Others flocked to the hot spots du jour. While business didn't grind to a halt, the restaurant was starting to lose money at a pace that was getting dangerous. In addition, Rick and his wife both agreed that the hours required of him to run a restaurant would give them no time to be together with the new baby.

Reluctantly, Rick decided to close his business. He sold the restaurant but because of the debt it had incurred, he received very little cash. That left him with the prospect of starting over with nearly $50,000 in personal credit card debt he had racked up over the last year.

While Rick's extensive contacts quickly led to a good sales job, the pay wasn't enough to make a dent in the credit card bills. Wanting to avoid bankruptcy at all costs, he found a company that offered to negotiate settlements of his debts. Rick entered the program and in two years the credit card debts were all negotiated and paid off. By then he was earning a steady income and was able to start saving money for a down payment on a new home. They'd need a larger place, after all, with another child on the way.

As this case illustrates, debt settlement can work. Contrast this with our next case...

Debt Elimination

Have you seen the ads arguing that our credit/banking system is illegal? The ads claiming that because of this illegality you can wipe out all your debts? Are you tempted?

Debt from Thin Air

Bernice and Bill were having money troubles. They were feeding their children but were falling behind on the mortgage. Bill drove a big rig and with gas prices up and freight hauling down he was having trouble making ends meet.

Bernice's mother Gladys was saddened by this situation. She had always wanted the best for her daughter and grandchildren. Gladys tried to get money to Bernice to help when she could. But Gladys was living close to the edge on a monthly basis herself and couldn't afford to consistently bail out Bernice and Bill.

Bill's father George was also troubled by the problems. But rather than give money, George sought to give advice. He suggested that Bill find someone to live in the house who could make the payments. Bill and family could move into a cheaper place they could afford, the renter of Bill's existing house could pay the mortgage and in a few years when Bill was in a better financial condition he could move back into the house and not lose the equity he was building in it.

Bill was not in the mood to take anyone's money or anyone's advice. He was angry at himself but more and more he was angry at the system.

He was angry that the taxes he paid were squandered on lazy workers and stupid programs. He was angry at the oil companies for their price manipulation. He was angry that the payroll taxes he had to pay went for Social Security and Medicare. The entire country knew they would never receive the benefit of that money, so why did everyone keep blindly paying into the system?

More and more Bill believed the system was stacked against him. And then Joe, a friend at work, told him about Debt Elimination.

Joe indicated there were a number of sites on the internet that told the truth about America's banking system. By doing a search under the headings Debt Elimination or Mortgage Elimination Joe said he would find the sites where the dark truths would be revealed.

Bill spent several hours on the Internet learning what he knew in his heart. The American banking system was a fraud. It created money out of thin air.

At one site, Sentinel Counselors for American Mortgages, Bill learned that he didn't have to pay his mortgage. This was because his mortgage was not a loan but an exchange. Bill had given the bank a promissory note to pay $100,000. The bank deposited that as an asset. Thus, the bank owes him $100,000 because they are treating Bill's promise to pay as an asset by their own bookkeeping.

Bill was very excited by this information and told Bernice triumphantly that they didn't have to pay their mortgage.

Bernice was confused. The $100,000 they borrowed went to the previous owners for his property. How could they get out of paying that?

Because, Bill argued, the bank had never created a loan. Their promissory note was a bookkeeping entry that allowed the bank to create the appearance of a loan. But in fact no true money had been used. It was all pretend.

Bernice still didn't understand. Even if their promissory note was all pretend for accounting purposes, they had received an actual house in return. It had three bedrooms, two baths and a nice kitchen. It wasn't pretend to her.

Bill became agitated. He said it was usury to pay interest on pretend loans, loans created out of thin air. The loan he had entered into did not involve monies backed by gold or silver or something real. The loan was instead propped up by people's valueless and worthless faith in the system.

Bernice was still confused. If people had faith in the system, didn't that in and of itself create value? If everyone agrees to pay back what they borrow doesn't everyone benefit by being able to borrow?

Bill became very angry at her lack of understanding of the manipulative system that made people slaves to America's banks. He returned to the Sentinel Counselors of American Mortgages website to sign up for their debt elimination program. By paying $1,500 he would have the exclusive use of a counselor trained in debt elimination. They would show him how to fill out the forms necessary to eliminate his debt.

The counselor on the phone congratulated Bill on his decision and reiterated that no legitimate debt had been created. The bank took his promise to pay $100,000 and made it into an asset – an asset the bank had to repay. Since there was no loan created but only an exchange with the bank, the forms he filled out would negate the exchange and free him from false debt.

After their first mortgage payment went unpaid, Bernice got a call from the bank. The mortgage was overdue and they needed to make a payment. Bernice mumbled an excuse, then immediately told Bill.

Bill told Bernice not to worry. He was in the process of eliminating the debt.

Bernice started sobbing. Why had he done that? It didn't make sense to begin with and now they were going to lose their home.

Bill raised his voice. They were not going to lose their home. Once the paperwork was processed the mortgage would be cancelled and the debt eliminated. America's fraudulent bankers would be off their backs.

Bernice pleaded with him. How could they possibly receive their $100,000 home for free? It wasn't fair or right to use some convoluted argument to get out of an obligation they had freely entered into two years ago. She didn't want the house if they were going to cheat people out of it.

Bill shouted they were going to own the house without fraudulent debt and stormed out of the house. He had a long haul to make and was already late.

When he returned, Bernice was preparing to move. The bank was threatening foreclose and Bernice had no money of her own to make the payments. She told Bill he could pack his own things. They would be living in different places.

Bill was furious. He called the debt elimination company demanding to know why his debt wasn't eliminated.

The representative on the phone was very glib. The debt was already eliminated because it never existed at the start.

Then why, Bill demanded, was he losing his house?

The representative calmly explained that the banking system illegally maintained improper control of the courts and the legal system. While the debt was not real the banks had the ability to enforce their fraud through the corrupt use of legal power.

Bill was angry. That was a nice smooth answer he fumed but it didn't get him his house back. He had paid $1,500 to have the debt eliminated. He didn't want excuses.

The representative insisted that they had no control over the court system. The only assisted with the necessary paperwork. Dealing with the corrupt use of power and illegal taking of homes was beyond the scope of their services.

Bill demanded his $1,500 back. The representative said that was impossible. They had helped him fill out the two one-page forms. Sentinel Counselors of American Mortgages had earned their fee.

Bill was now distraught. He had lost his wife and was about to lose his home. He called his father and told him the whole story.

While supportive and calming George said he should have known the outcome from the start.

Bill wanted to know why.

His father asked him to repeat the company name and identified their acronym: "SCAM".

The lesson of this story is to stay away from Debt Elimination and Mortgage Elimination programs. The only help they provide is to help themselves to your money and help you get into deeper trouble.

Bankruptcy

The word bankruptcy alone can conjure a range of emotions including shame, disapproval, and fear. If you've been through a bankruptcy, you may wish it never happened. If you haven't ever had to file, you may judge those who have as simply irresponsible with their finances. The truth is, common life events such as divorce, a small business that goes under, a lawsuit, or an unexpected illness can throw anyone's financial life into a tailspin and land them in bankruptcy court.

According to research on families and bankruptcy by then Harvard Law Professor Elizabeth Warren nobody is immune from the possibility of bankruptcy. Bankruptcy occurs in all walks of life and income levels. "The data show that families filing for bankruptcy... were a cross section of middle-class America," she explains. Warren has reported bankrupt debtors to be:

- At an educational level slightly higher than average in the U.S.
- About a 50/50 mix of homeowners and renters.
- Employed in fields that mirror the range of occupations in the U.S. job market.

In addition:

About 90% would be classified as "solidly middle class."

- Two out of three debtors had lost a job at some point shortly before filing.
- Nearly half had medical problems.
- One-fifth of the debtors had recently been through a divorce.

In fact, Warren says that jobs, medical problems, and divorce account for about 80% of the filings.

Her scariest statistic, however, is this: The single greatest predictor that a woman will file bankruptcy is whether she has children.

What happens in bankruptcy?

Currently, most people file under Chapter 7 of the bankruptcy code. This is often called "straight bankruptcy." In a Chapter 7 filing, some or all debts are discharged (or written off). In exchange, the debtor may lose property that was not "exempt" from bankruptcy.

The process usually takes some 60 to 90 days, and after it's completed, debtors can begin to rebuild their financial lives. While these consumers will pay higher rates for credit, and find it more difficult to reestablish credit, they are able to start over again when their bankruptcies are completed.

A smaller percentage of consumers file under Chapter 13 of the bankruptcy code. This is often called a "wage earner's plan." In a Chapter 13 filing, the consumer agrees to pay back a portion of his or her debts under a court-ordered plan administered by a bankruptcy trustee. Chapter 13 is chosen when a consumer wants to make a good faith effort to pay back debts, when he or she doesn't qualify for a Chapter 7, or because there are some assets the debtor wants to keep, but would lose under a Chapter 7 plan.

Debtors typically are not able to begin rebuilding their credit until the bankruptcy plan is completed, but there is a bright side: Chapter 13 bankruptcies are voluntarily removed from credit reports 7 years after filing, while Chapter 7 bankruptcies are reported for 10 years from filing.

A few things to understand about bankruptcy:

1. Bankruptcy can stop collection efforts, giving you time to deal with your debts. But even a Chapter 7 won't erase all debts. For example, you'll still have to deal with student loan payments, most tax debts, child support and spousal support. While foreclosure may be postponed, you'll still have to be able to pay your mortgage and

catch up on your payments if you want to keep your home. Your attorney can give you more details.

2. You'll have to pay attorney's fees and filing fees, which can add up to a few thousand dollars. While some companies will offer to help you do it on your own, it's best to get an attorney if you can because it is increasingly difficult to navigate the complex process yourself.

3. If you have co-signed debts and you file for bankruptcy but the other borrower doesn't, they will be on the hook for the entire debt.

If you think bankruptcy may become inevitable, it's better that you meet with an attorney sooner rather than later to discuss it. Many people make costly mistakes that they could have avoided if they understood the facts. One prime example we previously pointed out: Raiding retirement funds to pay bills, then ending up in bankruptcy anyway. Those retirement funds may have been protected from creditors. It is better to go into bankruptcy with retirement funds you can keep once the process is concluded.

Stress and Debt

According to a survey by Myvesta, almost half of people with problem debt can be classified as depressed. Of those, just under 40 percent reported symptoms of severe depression. In comparison, studies have shown that 9.5 percent of the general population is clinically depressed.

This means if you are struggling with debt you may first need to make an appointment with a mental health counselor or your doctor to try to get any clinical depression under control. It's pretty difficult to take charge of your financial life when just getting through the day is a challenge. In addition, as we mentioned in the first chapter, some studies have found medication that can help those with compulsive spending problems.

The Costly Mistake

The biggest mistake people make when they are deep in debt is to procrastinate. It's the "deer in the headlights" syndrome, and credit counselors and bankruptcy attorneys see it all the time. It's painfully obvious to everyone except the person in debt that they need to make a hard choice or they won't have many choices left.

The other response is what financial expert Steve Rhode of GetOutofDebt.org calls "magical thinking." Americans by and large are an optimistic lot. We buy lottery tickets and spend tomorrow's income today, and well before the ship comes in. At the same time, that can be a costly mistake when it comes to getting out of debt.

As Elizabeth Warren says in her enlightening book, *The Two Income Trap:* "The greatest danger for a family in financial distress is not bill collectors (although they can be the most annoying). The greatest danger is false optimism. We heard it over and over again in our interviews (for their study of bankruptcy): "We thought Mark would be back at work right away... We didn't think Grandpa could go on like this much longer." These families knew they had been hit by a disaster but they didn't respond fast enough because they thought it would pass quickly."

Don't let debt scare you into doing nothing. You know your options. Act now to get the help you need so you can focus your time and energy on creating a positive financial future.

Part Two

Emergency Measures for Crisis Debt Situations

Chapter Seven

Car Loan Troubles

Vehicles are expensive. It's not uncommon for a new vehicle to cost $30,000 or more – and luxury vehicles can cost much more. The average loan now takes more than five years for borrower to pay off.

What does this mean to you? It means that you, like many people, may be upside down on your car, owing more than it's worth. It means that if you do decide you want to get rid of your car you'll have no choice but to get into a more expensive loan, one that pays off the new car and the remaining balance of the old one.

It may also mean that the payments that were affordable when you took your loan, may not be so easy to make now – especially if your income has gone down or if you've had expensive car repairs. And let's not forget the increasing price for a gallon of gas.

If you are having trouble keeping up with expensive car loan payments, here are several options to consider:

Refinance It: Many people don't realize that car loans can be refinanced just like other types of loans. The best time to refinance is before you fall behind. Even if you have less than perfect credit, though, you may be able to find a lender that will refinance you.

Sell It: If you're not upside down, meaning you owe less than your car is worth, you may just want to sell it and find something cheaper in the meantime. You're certainly better off doing this than having it repo'd and sold at an auction for far less than you may get on your own. You may also be able to get the lender to agree to let a creditworthy borrower take over the loan but it may take some negotiating. If you've leased your vehicle, you may be able to get out of your lease using a website like LeaseTrader.com or Swapalease.com.

Work It Out: If you've had your car loan for at least six months (and made those payments on time), your lender may be willing to work out a modified payment schedule for you. There are several ways they can do this, including letting you skip a payment or two and tack them onto the end of the loan, or allowing you to make smaller payments for a few months then getting back on track. In some cases, the entire loan can be modified. It depends on your situation and the lender's policies. But you won't know if you don't ask.

It is essential that you get any agreements from your creditor in writing. And don't assume anything. You may assume, for example, that by agreeing to your lower payments, the lender won't report you as late to the credit reporting agencies. Your assumption may be wrong. Be forewarned and negotiate as much as you can.

Turn It In: In a voluntary repossession, you turn in the car and save the lender the repossession costs. It can still be reported on your credit report (and will be considered seriously negative) but that may be negotiable too. Talk to your lender if this is your only option. If you show a hardship situation, they may be willing to work with you.

Get Help: What if you can't work it out? Or if your income is unstable or low, and unlikely to pick up? If your car is vital for getting to your job, or getting the kids to school or child care, for example, you may want to focus paying that loan first and letting other bills (like credit cards) slide until you can catch up. Or by using the advice in the previous chapter and working with a reputable counseling agency or debt settlement firm, you may be able to cut your other bills so you can keep up with the essential ones.

Bankruptcy may be another option. If you file, you may be able to keep your car without having to catch up on those payments that are behind right now. And in some situations you may be able to just pay off the current value of the car (as opposed to the full loan) as well as stretch out your payments. For more information, talk with a bankruptcy attorney.

Vehicle Repossession

If you fall behind on your car loan or lease, the lender (or lessor) may have the right to repossess your vehicle. Each state has its own laws, but in many states repossession can happen quickly, without any advance notice or permission from the court. Plus, the lender may have the right to sell your loan contract to a third party, who can also repossess the vehicle if you fall behind or otherwise default on your contract.

There are some limits on repossessions, however, and if the lender violates rules you may be entitled to damages.

Falling Behind

Many people mistakenly think that even if they fall behind on their car loan or lease, as long as they are paying something it can't be repossessed. They also may think that their car can't be repo'd unless they fall at least 90 days behind. That usually is not true.

The contract you signed when you took out the loan will spell out the definition of "default." Failing to pay on time one time may put you in default. Letting your insurance lapse may do the same. In addition, the fact that you are in default may allow some lenders to "accelerate" your loan, or ask for the full balance immediately. In some states, lenders must notify you when you are in default and give you the opportunity to catch up before they can take your vehicle.

While lenders can usually go onto your property to take your car, they usually can't commit what's called a "breach of the peace." This may include:
- Removing your car from a closed or locked garage without your permission
- Using physical threats or force to take your car

It is often legal, however, for the repo man to come onto your property to take your car; or hotwire your car or use a duplicate key to take it.

If you had any items in the vehicle when it was taken, you're usually entitled to get them back. But you may have to claim them quickly (sometimes within 24 hours) so don't delay if your vehicle was repo'd and you had items of value inside.

Your state attorney general's office should be able to give you information about state vehicle repossession laws. Visit the naag.org website for a referral to your state attorney general's office. Lenders who breach the peace in seizing your car may be required to compensate you if they harm you or your property.

Repo Sales

When your car is repossessed, it will usually be sold. While it is usually sold at a public auction, some states allow private sales as well. You always have the right to redeem your vehicle before it's sold by paying the full balance due plus any associated costs and fees. (Of course, if you could afford to do that it's unlikely it would have lost it in the first place.)

In other states, the law is more consumer-friendly. In those states, you can reinstate the loan if you can pay the amount you're behind plus late fees, repossession costs and related expenses (such as attorney fees). This too can be tough if you're already behind, but you may be able to work out a temporary arrangement with a friend or relative who can lend you the money to catch up. Of course you'll have to keep up with your payments then or risk losing your vehicle again.

If your car is sold, then whatever the sale brings, minus allowable expenses for repossessing and selling the car, will be applied toward your loan balance. These public auctions usually do not bring top dollar, so you'll likely be billed for the difference, or the deficiency. For example, say you owe $15,000 on your car, and it's sold at auction for $10,000 and there were $1,500 in costs for the repossession and sale, there would be a deficiency of $6,500.

If you can't pay the deficiency, the lender will likely turn that balance over to a collection agency or may sue to get a deficiency judgment. That means your headaches still aren't over when the vehicle is gone. You may well have no vehicle, a damaged credit record, and still be hassled for the balance.

In addition, if you can't pay the deficiency and the lender is unsuccessful in collecting it from you, the lender may send you (and the IRS) a tax form 1099-C reporting the unpaid balance. The IRS considers this "forgiven debt" as income and will expect you to pay taxes on it unless you can show that you are insolvent. We'll discuss the whole issue of forgiveness of debt is income further up ahead.

Back to the repossession of cars. If your car is sold, it must be sold in a "commercially reasonable manner." Again, that doesn't mean it has to be sold for top dollar, but it can't be sold for a rock bottom price so that the seller can work out a side agreement and pocket the difference. Many auctioned vehicles are sold at dealer auctions and the dealers are going to bid a low enough price to be able to resell the vehicle and still make a profit.

If you think your repo'd vehicle may not have been sold in a commercially reasonable manner, it would be a good idea to talk with your state attorney general's office and a consumer law attorney in your area.

Cosigners beware. If you cosigned for a vehicle and the other borrower didn't pay, you'll face the same consequences as the original borrower. And in most cases, the lender doesn't even have to notify the co-signer that the loan is delinquent.

Example: John cosigned a loan for his father-in-law, who needed the vehicle to get to work. His father-in-law couldn't keep up on the payments when he fell ill, and the truck was repo'd. John didn't know about the problem with the truck, and his father-in-law died soon after.

Three years later, John started receiving collection calls about a $20,000 deficiency balance on the truck. He couldn't afford to pay it, but managed to keep the debt collectors at bay for a couple of years. Finally, after the collectors gave up, he received a notice that the balance was reported to the IRS as "Discharge of Indebtedness Income." Remember, when a debt is discharged (they stop trying to collect) it is as if you have 'earned' the amount forgiven. As a result, John was forced to pay taxes as if he had received that $20,000 in income.

If you are being dunned for a vehicle you cosigned for, try to work out a reasonable settlement with the lender – and talk to your tax advisor. (See the section on debt collectors for more advice.)

But now let's look at one of the biggest debts you'll ever take on...

Chapter Eight

Mortgage Troubles

In the first decade of the 21st century, many Americans thought of their homes as ATM's or "can't lose" investments. In the second decade, these same homes have turned into prisons – keeping homeowners trapped, often in homes that are underwater. What if you already have a mortgage and are having trouble keeping up with the payments? This isn't unusual: In fact, in 2012, an estimated two million will go into foreclosure, and almost one in four homes with a mortgage is in negative equity, which means the value of the home is less than what's owed on it. By some estimates, it will take decades to clear out all the current and future foreclosure cases. Of course, this will weigh on real estate prices for years to come. Knowing that, be realistic about your situation.

If you're falling behind on your mortgage it's important to get a plan together quickly and act on it. You should have two goals here:

1. To make a good decision about what to do with your home. This may be harder than you think since lenders have done a good job of making this sound like a moral decision, rather than a business one. Getting all the facts – and solid advice – can help you make a better decision here.

2. Minimize the financial fallout from whatever option you choose. Your goal is to make the best decision you can, accept the consequences, then move forward with your wealth-building plans without another financial disaster (taxes, a lawsuit) hanging over your head. That's the credit winner's approach.

Many good, hardworking, honest people lose their home to foreclosure and one of the main reasons is that they simply refuse to acknowledge that they are in trouble. They keep waiting or hoping for a solution to bail them out, and it doesn't. It's easy to feel overwhelmed and afraid. But waiting to find a solution will be expensive, and will narrow your options. If you're in trouble, work on a solution now.

How the foreclosure works depends on which state you live in, and can take a very short time or as long as a year and a half or more.

If you do lose your home to foreclosure, and the foreclosing lender gets less than is owed (plus expenses) from the sale, there is a deficiency. For example, if you owed $100,000 on your mortgage and the lender incurred $7,000 in expenses foreclosing and selling the property, then received only $90,000 in the sale, there is a deficiency of $17,000. ($100,000 + 7,000 - $90,000). If there is a deficiency, you may face two nasty surprises:

1. The lender may have to report this "forgiven" amount to the IRS on a 1099-C, and you'll be expected to pay taxes on it as if it were income to you. If that's the case, make sure you talk with a tax advisor who may be able to help you wipe out that tax debt if you qualify. We'll talk more about this later in the book.

2. The lender may sue you for the deficiency – the difference between what you owed plus expenses and what they received in the sale of the property. That means that you may still have a lender trying to collect from you even after the foreclosure. As of this writing, these lawsuits aren't terribly common, but that doesn't mean that won't change in the future as lenders start selling the balances to debt collection firms. If you had a second loan, or other liens on the property and the lender with the first mortgage forecloses, you may have two lenders pursuing you for a deficiency.

3. Tax liens must be paid before the property can be sold again.

There are times when letting a home go into foreclosure is the best of several bad options. But in many cases, proactively pursuing an alternative to foreclosure allows to you to put the mess behind you. Here are some strategies:

Catch up on your payments: In some states, you can stop the foreclosure by paying the amount you are behind plus any other fees due. In some states, this does *not* stop the lender from foreclosing. Of course, if you could do this you might not be in trouble in the first place.

Sell: If the market is strong and you have enough equity in your home to pay the closing costs associated with a sale, you may be best off selling your home. The lender may even put your foreclosure on hold for a little longer to allow you to do that. Be sure to get any agreements from the lender to that effect in writing.

If you are behind on your payments, think twice about trying to sell your home "by owner" or with a part-time agent to save on the real estate commission. If you are pressed for time, your best bet is to get a full-time agent with an excellent track record who will price and market your home aggressively for a fast sale. Also watch out for real estate agents who throw out a high sales figure just to get your listing. You need to be realistic in your expectations, and get the house sold before you lose it.

Let Someone Take Over Your Payments: If your payments are reasonable for the area, but you don't have enough equity to sell your home, you may be able to sell it to a buyer "subject to" the current mortgage. In other words, they take over your mortgage payments and then refinance the loan to pay you off at an agreed upon time in the future. You may also be able to get a little cash out of the deal to move to another place. This can keep you out of foreclosure and keep the mortgage in good standing.

There are two caveats here. First, most loans today are not assumable. That means you really can't allow someone to just assume your mortgage. The loan contract usually contains an acceleration clause that allows them to call the entire loan due if they learn the house has been sold subject to the mortgage. As long as they are getting their monthly payments, most lenders won't enforce a due on sale clause, but you should be aware of the risk.

The second warning is a serious risk. There are people who prey on homeowners in pre-foreclosure. They use a variety of tactics to essentially buy your home very cheaply. One of these schemes is equity skimming, in which the "buyer" offers to take care of your financial troubles by putting someone in your home. They will often have you deed the house over to them, then promise to make the mortgage payments. They collect rent but don't pay your mortgage so you end up in foreclosure anyway.

Another is a fraudulent sale/leaseback arrangement where the investor agrees to buy your home and lease it back to you. You are promised that in a year or so your credit will be repaired and you'll be able to buy the home back. But the terms of the deal are usually so onerous that you end up losing the house – often at a ridiculously low price.

That doesn't mean that working with an investor to help you find a way to keep you out of foreclosure is always a bad option. In some cases, it may be your best option for preventing your foreclosure. But since this is an emotional and complicated transaction, be careful. Choose an experienced investor to work with.

Rent It: If your monthly payment is attractive, you may be able to find a renter who can cover your payments while you work out your financial difficulties. This is risky for you, of course, because if the renter can't – or doesn't – pay, you'll be trying to evict them while scrambling to keep your home. If you consider this option, make sure you hire a company to do a full background check on your tenant, get a healthy deposit plus first and last month's rent, and consider using a management company to manage the property for a monthly fee.

Give It Back: With a "deed in lieu of foreclosure," you save the lender time and money by avoiding the foreclosure process. Essentially you deed your house back to the lender. While a deed in lieu can be reported on your credit report (and can be a seriously negative mark), you may be able to negotiate with the lender not to report it. Keep in mind that if you have a second mortgage or home equity line of credit, deeding it back to the lender does not wipe out the second loan. Just because you don't have the home anymore does not mean the lenders cannot try to collect on the second.

Note: You may be asked on future mortgage loan applications whether you have ever transferred title back to a lender to avoid foreclosure so even if it's not on your credit report, it may come up again.

Also note that you can't simply send your keys back to your lender. In many cases, lenders already have too many REO properties in their inventory, and they don't want your home. If you want to try this route, be sure to work with an attorney with experience in helping homeowners in distress. The attorney will help you negotiate a deed-in-lieu and make sure all the paperwork is completed so the home is officially transferred back to the bank.

Refinance It: If you have equity in your home, you may be able to refinance it out of pre-foreclosure. It can be tricky, though, and the last thing you want to do is waste your time with a mortgage lender or broker who promises you the world then can't get the loan. Also watch out for very high interest rates or prepayment penalties that will make it difficult to sell if you need to. When you're desperate to save your home, you may be willing to do just about anything but predatory loans can make matters worse. Make sure you're dealing with a broker or lender who has actually helped consumers in trouble, and don't let them drag it out too long.

Short Sale It: If you owe close to what your home is worth – or more than it's worth – you may be able to get the lenders to agree to a short sale. You'll need a buyer for your home (no, it cannot be a relative) and this is probably best done with a real estate professional with experience in short sales, or an investor who already has successfully done short sales, simply because they'll know how to negotiate with the lender.

Example: Let's say your home is worth around $80,000 and you owe about $75,000. Even if you sold if for the full $80,000, your closing costs and real estate commissions would put you in the hole – which you can't afford since you're already behind. In addition, if you've fallen behind on your mortgage, you've probably put off other repairs and the house probably isn't in tip-top condition.

A savvy real estate investor may work out a deal with the bank to pay them off at $65,000 and give you a little money to help you move. The bank gets more than they probably would in a foreclosure, and you avoid a foreclosure (and avoid a possible deficiency judgment) and head to your new place.

Always make sure you have a real estate attorney review your paperwork before you sell your home this way. You want to make certain that the lender won't be able to come back to you for a deficiency years later.

Work It Out: The lender may agree to modify your loan to allow you to catch up. Some of the modifications that can be worked out include:

- Tack the payments you are behind on to the end of the loan.
- Allow you to catch up on the missed payments by adding them to your current payments for a few months.
- Allow you to pay only interest, plus any escrows for taxes and insurance for a period of time.
- Reduce your interest rate and penalties

Understand that the lender is going to want to see details of your financial situation both to support the fact that you are in a hardship situation, as well as to show that you will be able to get caught up and pay in the future. A workout would not be a realistic option, for example, if you have taken a significant cut in pay and have not secured extra income that would allow you to keep up with your bills.

Mortgages and Members of the Military

If you serve in the military you have some rights (as you should). The Soldiers' and Sailors' Civil Relief Act (SCRA) of 1940 and the more recent Service Members Civil Relief Act of 2003 which updated and expanded that older law, helps protect active military and their families from foreclosure. While you will still have to pay your loan, the SCRA provides for the temporary cessation of foreclosure and other collection actions.

Will the SCRA protect you? Yes if:

1. You are on active duty or are a co-signer or dependent of an active duty member,
2. You or your dependents still own the property,
3. The debt was arranged prior to active duty and is secured by a deed of trust or mortgage,
4. The lender has started foreclosure proceedings, and
5. Your ability to pay the loan has been materially affected by your military service.

If you qualify you can use the SCRA to reduce your interest rate and thus your payments. Once you are called up to active duty, and are theoretically making less money, you should ask for the interest rate reduction. Don't wait until there is a problem. You can write your lender a letter asking that the interest rate be reduced. Send the letter by certified mail, return receipt requested.

If a lender ignored your request and forecloses (or forecloses for any reason) the SCRA gives you the right to stop the proceeding. Notify the lender that you are on active duty. Most lenders know that courts will sanction them (that is assess monetary fines) for foreclosing on an active duty owner and will stop. If your lender still continues, the SCRA gives you the right to file a lawsuit to stop the foreclosure.

If you need a lawyer to help you with such matters there are resources available to you at the office of the unit judge advocate or installation legal assistance officer. We will talk more about additional rights you have under the SCRA later in this book.

File Bankruptcy: Filing bankruptcy can stall a foreclosure, but it does not wipe out your mortgage debt. Depending on your state's laws, how far you are behind and what type of bankruptcy you file, you'll still have to be able to work out a payment arrangement to catch up on your mortgage and then continue to make your payments going forward. Sometimes, however, the stall is what you need to be able to sell your house or get an investor to buy it in a short sale situation (the court's permission will be required). In other situations, a bankruptcy can wipe out other debts making it possible for you to keep up with the mortgage payment.

And now, let's further your education...

Chapter Nine

Student Loans

Today's students need to graduate with degrees in debt management.
While credit card debt among students is a growing problem, it's often tiny compared to the problem of student loan debt. Higher education costs are now so high that many students have no choice to borrow. And they often borrow as much as they can, assuming that they'll be have no trouble paying the loan back when they start working and earning a salary.

The average student graduates with over $20,000 in student loans. After graduate school it can be as high as $200,000 for some students. Why are these numbers so high? First, colleges and universities have become extremely wasteful, just like the federal government. They employ far too many bureaucrats who add nothing to the educational dynamic. Second, many students (and their parents) also assume a higher education will "pay off" with a higher salary or perks, regardless of the field they are entering. It's not unusual for would-be school teachers or social workers, for example, to graduate with student loan debt of $30,000 or more, only to face starting salaries of just over $30,000, or no jobs at all.

Falling behind on a student loan can be very expensive. The collection costs can be very high, in addition to the interest you may already be paying. Unlike other debts where collectors have only a certain number of years to sue you, federal student loan debts can haunt you for years and years. (Private student loans are subject to the statute of limitations.) Also, it is extremely difficult to discharge most student loans in bankruptcy.

In addition, you will have trouble getting student loans in the future, your income tax refund may be seized, you may be subject to wage garnishment without first being taken to court, and you will find it difficult to catch up as well as pay off that student loan debt in the future.

However, there is some good news. If you are in default on a federal loan and enter a loan rehabilitation program, then make twelve consecutive on-time payments you can bring your loan out of default. (Note, you can't be one day late on those payments.) When you do, your previous late payments will be removed from your credit report. Another option for getting out of default is to find out whether it is possible to consolidate your student loan out of default. See the Resources section for more information.

If you have complaints about how your Direct Loans, Federal Family Education Loans (FFEL), Guaranteed Student Loans, and Perkins Loans have been handled, and cannot resolve the problem with the lender, contact the Department of Education's Student Loan Ombudsman Office at (877) 557-2575.

Here are some additional strategies that Gerri Detweiler, our contributing editor, has found helpful for coping with high levels of student loan debt:

Cancellation: Student loans may be cancelled in part or in full for any of the following:

- Total and Permanent Disability: Loans may be discharged if a doctor certifies that you are totally and permanently disabled and unable to work or earn money.

- School Closure: If you received a student loan at a school that closed before you completed your studies, you may be eligible for discharge of your loan.

- Ability to Benefit: Your loan can be discharged if the school admitted you based on your ability to benefit from the training but you weren't properly tested to measure that ability or you failed the test.

- Child and Family Services Cancellation: You may be eligible to cancel your student loan if you are solely "providing or supervising the provision of services to high-risk children who are from low-income communities and the families of those children."

- Teacher Cancellation Discharge: You may be eligible to cancel your student loan if you are teaching full-time at a low-income school, as determined by your state's education agency; are a special-education teacher, including teachers of infants, toddlers, children, or youth with disabilities; or teach in the fields of mathematics, science, foreign languages, or bilingual education, or in any other field of expertise determined by a state education agency to have a shortage of qualified teachers in that state.

- Forged Signature: If you believed that someone forged your signature on the loan application, promissory note, or authorization for electronic funds transfer, you may qualify for a loan discharge.

- School Owes You a Refund: You may also qualify for partial discharge of an FFEL or Direct Loan if your school failed to pay a tuition refund required under federal law.

- Death: If you die with an outstanding student loan, your federal student loan debt will be discharged. Your estate will not owe any money on your loan.

Deferment: Deferment allows you to temporarily postpone payments on your loan. Whether or not you will have to pay interest on the part of your loan that is deferred depends on the type of loan you have. Eligible reasons for deferment typically include economic hardship or unemployment, military deployment, enrollment in school or an internship program, etc. Since programs change, you'll want to check with your lender or the student loan websites in the Resources section to find out if deferment is an option.

Forbearance: If you are temporarily unable to meet your repayment schedule but are not eligible for a deferment, you may receive forbearance for a limited and specified period – usually for up to twelve months at a time for a total of thirty-six months. During forbearance, your payments are postponed or reduced. Whether your loans are subsidized or unsubsidized, you will be charged interest.

It is very important that you contact your lender about deferment or forbearance before you fall behind on your payments. If you wait until you are behind, you may not be eligible. Continue making your payments until your deferment is approved.

If you are approved for student loan forbearance or deferment, it should not be reported negatively on your credit reports, and should not hurt your credit scores.

Graduated repayment plan: With one of these plans, your payments start out low and will rise over time. This plan is often good for a student who is just staring out and expects their salary to increase, as they gain more experience. Caution: One of these plans can stretch your loan out to as long as thirty years.

Extended repayment plan: An extended repayment plan allows you to pay your student loan over 12-30 years instead of the standard ten-year plan. It is more expensive, but if the lower payments keep you out of default, it may be worth it.

Income contingent plan: With one of these plans, your payment is based on adjusted based on your adjusted gross income (AGI)—as reported on your U.S. income tax return—your family size, the interest rate, and the total amount of your Direct Loan debt.

Consolidation: If you have more than one student loan, you may be able to consolidate it into a lower cost single-payment loan. This can save you money if the new payment is lower than your previous combined payment, which is often the case because it is a new loan. Your consolidated student loan payment is based on the average interest rate on the student loans you are consolidating. Your consolidated rate is set by the government. So, there is not a whole lot of advantage in shopping around among different lenders.

In some cases, consolidating your student loan can also take you out of default, which can benefit you in a couple of ways. One way, of course, is by halting the collection costs associated with a defaulted student loan. The other way it can benefit you, is that it can help your credit report. If you make 12 consecutive on time payments, on a student loan that you have brought out of default, the previous late payments can be erased. For more information on consolidating student loans, see the Resources section.

Income Based Repayment: The Income Based Repayment (IBR) may offer some relief if you have federal student loans under the Direct Loan Program or the FFEL Program. If you qualify for IBR, your required monthly payment will be capped at an amount that is intended to be affordable based on your income and family size, and will be less than what you would have to pay under a 10-year Standard Repayment Plan.

After ten years of payments under IBR, you may be eligible for student loan forgiveness if you work in a field that qualifies for loan forgiveness under the Direct Loan Public Service Loan Forgiveness Program. You must work for a qualified non-profit or in another field that qualifies, including military service, law enforcement, public education or early childhood education, and other fields. For all other types of work, you may be eligible for forgiveness of the loan balance after twenty years of payments under IBR. Get details at IBRinfo.org.

Be a Smart Borrower

It's not unusual for student loans to be sold, or for a student to have eight or more loans. It can be tough keeping track of them all. Lose track of a loan, though, and you may quickly find yourself in student loan hell. The Department of Education offers these tips for being a smart borrower, and they're good ones:

Keep all your loan documents: This simple piece of advice is one of the most important. You'll have problems later if you can't find your promissory note, can't remember what type of loans you received, or don't know who you're supposed to repay or how you go about postponing (deferring) repayment if you should have financial difficulties. Keep a file of all documents connected with your loans from the time you first get a loan, so you'll always have what you need in one place. Then, you won't be confused about what you're supposed to do or who you're supposed to contact if you have questions. Even better: Scan copies of your documents and save them in an online storage service like DropBox, EverNote or Google Docs so you'll always have them, even if you somehow misplace your originals. (Keep the originals as well.)

Take Notes: Whenever you talk to your lender or loan servicer, keep a record of the person you talked to, the date you had the conversation, and what was said. If you send letters, always include your loan account number, and keep copies of those letters (and the responses you receive) in your file, and back it up online. That way, you'll know who said what and when, which can help you avoid problems and misunderstandings.

Notify: Tell your school and/or loan holder in writing if you move, change your name or Social Security Number, or reenroll in school. You must ensure your loan holder won't lose track of you. If that happens, you could miss payments and become delinquent (late). Also, your loan could be sold, and you won't know who has it or where to send payments because you couldn't be notified.

Ask questions: If there's something you don't understand or if you're having trouble making payments. Don't wait until things become too tough—ask for help from your loan holder or loan servicer right away.

Buck up. We're headed into tax territory...

Chapter Ten

When You Owe Taxes

Of any debt, tax debt is perhaps the most stressful. The IRS can be very aggressive in its collection efforts, and has strong, some may say extreme, powers that mere lenders don't, such as placing a lien on your property (or even seizing it), garnishing your wages, or seizing money from your bank account, all without going to court first. Tax liens are the only debt to remain on your credit report *forever* if they are not paid. If paid they still remain on your report for seven years from the date they are paid, though relatively new rules allow you to ask the IRS to remove a paid or satisfied tax lien from your credit report. We'll describe how that works later in the book.

If you owe the IRS money, whether it's a recent debt or one that's years old, it's time to figure out a way to settle up. Here are some options to consider:

Tap Your Savings: If you have money stashed away to pay the bill, do it. If you have some money saved but not enough for the entire bill, read the sections on repayment plans and offers in compromise.

Repayment Plan: You can ask the IRS for a repayment plan if you don't currently have an installment agreement in place and you have filed all required Federal tax returns. You file Form 9645 and request an affordable payment plan. If the IRS approves your plan, you'll pay a small fee plus interest. The interest rate is reasonable.

If your request is approved, you'll be able to pay your taxes in monthly payments instead of immediately paying the amount in full. In return, you'll need to make your monthly payments on time, and pay all your future tax liabilities. (That means you shouldn't adjust your withholdings so high that you'll end up with another tax bill you can't pay.)

Charge Them: You can pay your taxes with a credit card at the website officialpayments.com. The service charges a fee plus you'll pay interest on your credit card at the credit card companies' rate. It may not always be the cheapest way to go, but it can be better than letting interest and penalties continue to accrue.

Offer in Compromise: An Offer in Compromise is an agreement between a taxpayer and the IRS that resolves the taxpayer's tax debt. The IRS has the authority to settle, or "compromise," federal tax liabilities by accepting less than full payment under certain circumstances. It's considered a "last resort," but the IRS may be willing to accept an offer in compromise if there is:

- Doubt that the assessed tax is correct.
- Doubt that you could ever pay the full amount of tax owed.
- Extenuating circumstances such as the collection of the tax would create an economic hardship or would be unfair and inequitable.

You don't need a tax professional to prepare an Offer in Compromise, but it may be helpful depending on your circumstances.

File Bankruptcy: Bankruptcy generally does not wipe out tax debts, but there are situations where it can be used to eliminate older tax bills. Consult a bankruptcy attorney for advice. As I've mentioned elsewhere, it may eliminate other bills so you are able to pay off your tax debt and other essential bills.

Get Professional Help: If you have "fudged" things on your taxes, or have some questionable issues, hire a tax attorney to help you clean up the mess. CPA's and enrolled agents may be called to testify against you in tax court, but your communications with tax attorneys are protected by attorney client privilege.

Why the IRS Cares About Your Debt Troubles

I know that it sounds crazy and wrong, but the 'forgiveness of debt is income' issue does kind of make sense in a strange way. Suppose you borrowed $10,000 from a company and now you need to pay it back. You are struggling and the company in an unusual burst of magnificence lets you off the hook. They tell you, "You don't have to pay the $10,000 you owe us." As a result, you are suddenly $10,000 richer. It is as if you 'earned' the $10,000. Can you see where the IRS comes in here? If you earn $10,000, the IRS wants a piece of that. And so when you "earn" $10,000 by having a loan forgiven they want to get a piece of that, too. Accordingly, forgiveness of debt is income, and you can expect the IRS to tax you on it.

To further understand the IRS position it helps to think like a thief. What if a worker arranged with his boss to not receive a salary, but a 'loan'? A year later the boss forgives the loan because the worker just happened to help him out. The worker maintains he didn't really earn anything, he just had a loan forgiven. He further maintains he doesn't owe taxes. Well, if this worked, we'd all do it. And for that reason alone, the IRS taxes it.

Taxes on Forgiven Debt

If you settle a debt for less than you owe, or if the creditor writes it off, the lender may send the IRS a 1099-C which is used to report "discharge of indebtedness income." In fact, creditors are required to do this if the forgiven debt exceeds $600. You normally will be sent a copy of this too, but if you've moved it may not reach you. The IRS expects you to pay taxes on this "income." If, however, you qualify for an exclusion or exception, you may be able to get out of paying taxes on some or all of that income.

You'll be using Form 982 plus instructions from the IRS to walk you through this process. But it can be confusing. Just take a look at the title of that form, "Reduction of Tax Attributes Due to Discharge of Indebtedness (and Section 1082 Basis Adjustment)." So I recommend you work with a tax professional who can guide you through it. However, to give you an idea of what's involved, here is a list of the things you'll be looking at:

Canceled Debt that Qualifies for Exclusion from Gross Income:
1. Cancellation of qualified principal residence indebtedness.
2. Debt canceled in a Chapter 11 bankruptcy case.
3. Debt canceled due to insolvency.
4. Cancellation of qualified farm indebtedness.
5. Cancellation of qualified real property business indebtedness.

Canceled Debt that Qualifies for Exception to Inclusion in Gross Income:
1. Amounts specifically excluded from income by law such as gifts or bequests.
2. Cancellation of certain qualified student loans.
3. Canceled debt that if paid by a cash basis taxpayer is otherwise deductible.
4. A qualified purchase price reduction given by a seller.

Of these, one of the most commonly used is the bankruptcy exclusion. Debt wiped out in bankruptcy is not taxable. Keep in mind, though, if you settled a debt before you filed for bankruptcy, the bankruptcy exclusion won't apply to that debt.

Another common way to avoid taxes on forgiven debt is by demonstrating you were insolvent at the time the debt was settled. Being insolvent by IRS definitions means your liabilities (debts) were greater than your assets at the time. To find out if you qualify, total the value of all your assets and, separately, total your debts. Be sure to include all your debts, even if they can't be wiped out in bankruptcy (student loans, for example.) You are insolvent by the amount your debts exceed your assets.

For example: Your have $20,000 in assets but $40,000 in debt. You are insolvent by $20,000. As long as any creditors agree to forgive $20,000 or less in debt, you should not have to include that amount in your taxable income. But if you manage to get your creditors to settle your debts so that you wipe out $25,000 in debt, you will likely have to report $5000 of income from forgiven debt on your tax return.

Either way, you should fill out Form 982 to demonstrate to the IRS why you aren't including income reported on a 1099-C in your taxable income.

For America's service men and women there are a few additional matters...

Chapter Eleven

Military Matters

The plight of military personnel and their bills is nothing new. As early in our country's history as the Civil War, America's service men were faced with trying to handle civil matters while simultaneously serving their country. In an effort to protect the interests of the nation while protecting those of Northern service men, Congress passed a moratorium on civil actions brought against Union sailors and soldiers. The moratorium recognized that military personnel need to be able to concentrate on the work of fighting a war rather than worrying about bills back at home. At the same time, the moratorium recognized that military personnel were not always paid enough to take care of the bills that stacked up while they were away serving the needs of the country. In simplest terms, the moratorium established that any civil actions (breach of contract, bankruptcy, foreclosure, divorce proceedings and the like) brought against a service man were deferred until he returned home.

In 1918, the moratorium was brought back into effect for military personnel serving in World War I. The Soldiers' and Sailors' Civil Relief Act of 1918 was not as comprehensive as the Civil War moratorium, but it did protect active service members from bankruptcy, repossession of property, foreclosure and similar actions. After World War I, the act expired.

The Soldiers' and Sailors' Civil Relief Act of 1940 took the act of 1918 one step further by lifting the setting of an expiration date for the soldiers serving in World War II. Between 1918 and 2003, the act was amended 11 times to reflect military and societal changes.

On December 19, 2003, President Bush replaced the law by signing into effect the Service Members' Civil Relief Act (SCRA). The new act retains the intent of the 1918 and 1940 acts, while also taking into account the changes our world has seen in the years since.

The SCRA helps service personnel meet their legal and financial obligations while fulfilling their military duties. It is not meant to help service men and women ignore their obligations, but rather it is meant to ease their burdens during active service. For example, the SCRA allows service personnel to cancel vehicle leases if they are deployed for 180 days or more. After all, they won't be using the vehicle while they are serving their country; is it right that they be required to pay?

Similarly, service men and women with permanent change of station orders or deployed to a new location for 90 days or more have the right to terminate housing leases. Nor can a member of the service or his or her family be evicted from housing while the service member is on active duty unless certain conditions are met (court order, lease rents in excess of $2,400, etc.).

The SCRA offers service personnel an automatic 90-day stay in all judicial and administrative civil proceedings upon application. Additional stays may be requested as well. If an additional stay is denied, the court must appoint counsel to protect the rights of the service man or woman while he or she is on active duty.

The SCRA includes a 6 percent limit on interest rates for pre-service debts (including credit card debt). Any portion above 6 percent is not deferred, but permanently forgiven. After the service is complete, the service man or woman's monthly payments must reflect the amount of interest saved during the service period.

Service personnel in the Reserves are also protected under the SCRA from the time of their receipt of mobilization orders. This is meant to give them time to get their affairs in order.

Any service man or woman who claims the rights ensured under the SCRA is also protected from discrimination for such claims. You can't be fired from your job or evicted from your house or denied credit because you apply for SCRA coverage.

In addition to service personnel, the SCRA extends protection to United States citizens serving with allied forces in capacities considered similar to military service. The act also extends protection to dependents of service personnel if their ability to comply is materially affected by the service man or woman's military service.

The SCRA offers a variety of provisions to protect service men and women called to active service or long-term deployment. Most protections require a show of material affect as a prerequisite. Any member of the service facing either of these situations should check with their unit judge advocate or installation legal assistance officer for more information and assistance.

Now let's take on an even bigger challenge...

Chapter Twelve

Debt Collectors

Debt collectors are in the business of doing one thing: Collecting money. Often feared and dreaded, they can be very aggressive and make your financial life very stressful. Knowing your rights when it comes to debt collectors, though, can relieve some of that stress and help you take care of those annoying accounts.

Debt After Death

Elena was grief stricken. Joseph, her husband of fifty years, had just passed away. He had worked to the end but Elena was not left in a good financial condition. They were living in a decrepit mobile home on the edge of town. When Joseph passed, she was to receive a small life insurance settlement of $2,000. Elena had another $1,000 in the bank. That was all she had. At age 88, she would somehow have to survive on that amount.

Two weeks after Joseph's passing, Elena received a card from XYZ Services, Inc. The company offered its deepest condolences on the death of her husband Joseph. The letter also brought up the $9,000 amount Joseph owed on a credit card.

Elena was confused. She had never known about this account. It wasn't in her name.

A day later the calls started. The people on the phone were very smooth. They offered their respects but then talked about Elena's need to make a 'morality payment' to clear up her late husband's debt. "You have been through tough times," they would say, "but we need to resolve this issue."

Elena explained that she was destitute. Her car had been repossessed. She couldn't work. She did not know how long she would be able to make the monthly mobile home park payment. She had no idea what would happen next. That did not deter the collectors.

The collection agency called Elena ten times a day. They learned that she would soon receive a $2,000 life insurance payment. They strongly suggested that to clear her husband's name she turn the $2,000 over to the agency. They would wipe out Joseph's $9,000 debt with a $2,000 payment and the matter would be resolved.

A neighbor in the mobile home park happened by when Elena was on the phone with a collection agent. He could hear the fear and anxiety in Elena's voice.

After the call he interceded. He learned that the credit card was in Joseph's name. That meant when Joseph died the debt was extinguished. Elena was under no obligation to pay. The neighbor had Elena talk to an attorney friend of his. After reviewing the case, the attorney, on Elena's behalf, sued the collection agency for harassment.

As the case shows, in most cases, when you die your debts die with you. Surviving family members are under no obligation to cover those debts.

If you co-sign on a loan for a mortgage or a credit card, the co-signer is still responsible. But when the loan is in the deceased party's name alone, as it was with Joseph in Elena's case, the survivors are off the hook. (Keep in mind, if you live in a community property state – Arizona, California, Idaho, Louisiana, Nevada, New Mexico, Texas, Washington, Wisconsin – you may be responsible for debts incurred by your spouse during your marriage.)

Does that stop collection agencies from pursuing collection? Of course not. They will use the arguments of morality and family obligation to get whatever they can out of you in your time of grief and weakness. Many will even say there is no legal requirement to pay but will continue to call until some sort of payment is made, or until you decide to talk to an attorney to make it stop (which is highly recommended).

Beware of agency callers who misrepresent the law. You may know that you are not obligated until the caller starts questioning how the decedent passed. Some collectors will argue that the particular cause of death – be it accident, old age, disease or suicide – means that you are still responsible. This is not true. The cause of death has no effect on responsibility.

What if the decedent (like Joseph, the person who passed) left an estate? In that case, the collectors can file a claim in probate to get paid. Like creditors in a bankruptcy, they may or may not receive anything. Once the probate is finalized, the collectors cannot pursue family members. If this happens speak to an attorney.

Know your rights. And know that some collection agencies will do and say whatever they please, whether legal or not, to get you to pay. They are on commission, after all, and could care less about you in your time of grief.

There is a federal law called the Fair Debt Collection Practices Act (FDCPA) that requires that debt collectors treat you fairly. It doesn't stop them from trying to collect, but it does place certain limits on how they can collect.

The FDCPA applies to personal, family, and household debts. Business debts are not covered by the FDCPA. But if you used a personal credit card for purchases that were used by your business, the collector isn't likely to know that and is likely to follow the FDCPA if you know your rights.

A debt collector is any person who regularly collects debts owed to others. This includes attorneys who collect debts on a regular basis. It generally only applies to outside debt collection agencies, and not to creditors collecting their own debts, though your state may have laws that apply to creditors.

When you are first contacted by a debt collector, you should do several things:

1. Get contact information for the debt collector, including a phone number and address. You're entitled to this information under the FDCPA.

2. Dispute the debt if you think it's incorrect. Write to the collection agency immediately disputing the debt and requesting verification. Send your letter certified mail, return receipt requested. You're entitled to this verification under the FDCPA. Unless you are certain that you owe the full debt, disputing it will place the debt under dispute and give you time to figure out your options.

3. Start a correspondence file to keep notes about all your contacts with the collection agency: Who called, what they said and what was agreed. Also keep copies of all written correspondence. If the collector acts improperly, you may have legal remedies.

4. Verify that the statute of limitations for collecting the debt has not expired. If it has, and the debt collector tries to sue you for the debt, you can raise the statute of limitations as a defense against the lawsuit. And if you tell them to stop contacting you about the debt, they must comply (see below).

5. Do not pay a collector anything until you have established the debt is legitimate and worked out a payment arrangement. Don't be bullied around.

Notification

Within five days after you are first contacted about a debt, the collector must send you a written notice telling you the amount of money you owe; the name of the creditor to whom you owe the money; and what to do if you dispute the debt.

Each state has laws that describe how long creditors or collection agencies can sue to collect various types of debts. These are called the statutes of limitations. In some states, for some types of debts, it can be as little as four years, while in others it can be twenty years or more. This is important information because it's not unusual for collection agencies to make a last ditch effort to try to collect a debt right before the statute of limitations has expired.

If you make a payment on a debt, it may extend or revive the statute of limitations. Let's say a collector contacts you about a ten-year old debt that was outside the statute of limitations. They can't sue you to collect (if they do, you can raise the statute of limitations as a defense against the lawsuit) and they can't report it to the credit reporting agencies. So there's not a lot they can do to collect, especially if you tell them to leave you alone (see below). But if you pay them – even a token payment – it may start the statute of limitations over again.

It's also important to understand that paying a collection agency something, even a token payment, does not stop them from taking legal action to collect the debt. Collectors may pressure you to pay something to show "good faith." If you really can't afford to pay the debt or if you believe the debt is incorrect, you may be better off just refusing and asking them to leave you alone until you can pay. Again, remember that making a payment – even a small one – may extend the statute of limitations.

Calling You

A collector may contact you in person, by mail, telephone, telegram, or fax. However, a debt collector may not contact you at inconvenient times or places, such as before 8 a.m. or after 9 p.m. your time, unless you say that's OK. A debt collector also may not contact you at work if the collector knows that your employer disapproves of such contacts. If you tell a collector that you're not allowed to take calls at work, make a note of that conversation. If they do it again, call an attorney.

Privacy

Collectors are not supposed to tell anyone who is not a cosigner on your debt about it, other than your spouse. They can call neighbors or employers to get your contact information, but that's about as far as they are allowed to go. They're not allowed to say that they are calling regarding a debt. And once they've found you, contacts to third parties must stop.

If you hire an attorney to represent you, the collectors should contact your attorney, not you. I have provided this service to clients who are being roughly hounded by debt collectors. Collectors don't talk tough to an attorney (at least not after the first minute), and my clients can get some sleep.

Harassment, False Statements and Unfair Practices

Anyone who has dealt with debt collectors for a while will discover that it's not unusual for them to lie and say just about anything to get you to pay. There are legal limits on what they can say and do, but most people don't know their rights and so they just put up with it.

Watch out for any of the following types of statements or actions by collectors. Keep notes. If it looks like they are illegally harassing you, making false statements, or engaging in unfair practices, contact a consumer law attorney for help.

Examples of harassment:

- Threats of violence or harm;
- Obscene or profane language; or
- Repeatedly using the telephone to annoy you.

Examples of false statements:

- Falsely implying that you have committed a crime; or that you will be arrested if you don't pay your debt;
- Falsely representing that they operate or work for a credit bureau;
- Misrepresenting the amount of your debt;
- Indicating that papers being sent to you are legal forms when they are not;
- Falsely implying that someone not responsible for the debt (usually a spouse or family member) will be responsible;

- Threatening action that they cannot take (garnishing your wages immediately without taking you to court, for example); or

- Indicating that papers being sent to you are not legal forms when they are.

Important: A collector may threaten to notify your employer and garnish your wages if you don't pay immediately. For almost every type of consumer debt (except taxes and some student loans) the collector or creditor must first take you to court and get a judgment, then get the court's permission to garnish your wages. Whether or not they will actually go to those lengths depends on a number of things including how much you owe and how likely they think they are to collect. But it's not something that can generally happen overnight. Be alert to false statements like that from collectors and write them down.

Bankruptcy: If you have successfully completed bankruptcy and received a discharge, most remaining debts will be wiped out in bankruptcy. That means you do not owe those creditors any more money. But that doesn't stop all of them. Some will still try to collect debts wiped out in bankruptcy, even though doing so is illegal. As soon as you are contacted by a creditor or debt collector trying to collect on a discharged debt, begin fighting their efforts.

Notify your attorney (if you have one) or the bankruptcy court of their illegal actions. An attorney may be more than happy to help you because the collector will have to pay your attorney's fees if you successfully sue them for violating the FDCPA.

Unfair practices

Debt collectors may not engage in unfair practices when they try to collect a debt. For example, collectors may not:

- Collect any amount greater than your debt, unless allowed by state law;

- Deposit a post-dated check prematurely;
- Take or threaten to take your property unless this can be done legally; or
- Contact you by postcard.

As Gerri and I both agree, never, *ever* send a postdated check to a debt collector. The risks are too great. If you knowingly bounce a check you can be subject to criminal penalties.

How to Stop a Debt Collector

If you send a letter to a debt collector asking them to stop contacting you, they must stop. But it won't stop them from taking legal action to collect the debt. You can still be sued. It may make sense to write a "cease and desist" letter (just a fancy name for a letter telling them to leave you alone) if:

- You believe the statute of limitations has expired (point that out in your letter).
- You truly don't have the money to pay it (include a succinct description of your hardship situation).
- The debt collector is pressuring you to the point of creating unhealthy stress or physical side effects.
- You really don't believe you owe the debt and figure a judge would side with you if it ends up in court (describe why you believe you don't owe the debt).

See the Resources section for a sample Cease and Desist letter.

Negotiating

Collection accounts can often be negotiated for pennies on the dollar, especially if you can come up with a lump sum payment quickly. Most people are uncomfortable with negotiating but it's one of the most important skills you can learn and hone. I recommend you start your negotiations about 20 cents on the dollar. The debt collector may insist that there is a minimum amount they can accept, and that may or may not be true. You don't know. So you have to negotiate just as hard as they do.

It's much easier for debt collectors to try to get you to pay more than for you to pressure them to take less because:

a. the more they collect, the more they are likely to be paid, so it affects their bottom line,

b. it's not as emotional for them as it is for you, and

c. they negotiate debts every day, you don't.

Two other things to keep in mind:

1. Don't agree to something you can't afford. If you can't afford what they are proposing, tell the debt collector you can't and state that you'll call back when you've pulled some more money together. If they start threatening you, keep written notes and tell them you'll call back at another time.

2. Always at least try to get them to agree to remove any negative items from your credit report in exchange for payment. They may not agree, but if they do, get that in writing first, before you pay. Note that just listing a collection account as "paid" on your credit report is unlikely to raise your score.

There are companies that will do this negotiating for you if you're too uncomfortable. See the Resources section.

Scared and Pressured

If you are being pressured by debt collectors and are scared of what they can do if you don't pay, it may be worthwhile to talk with a consumer law attorney about your rights. The first consultation is usually free, but be sure to ask. You'll find more information in the Resources section.

Get Help

If you think the collector may be violating the law, get help from a consumer law attorney with experience in the FDCPA. You have the right to sue a collector in a state or federal court within one year from the date the law was violated. If you win, you may recover money for the damages you suffered plus an additional amount up to $1,000. Court costs and attorney's fees also can be recovered. A group of people also may sue a debt collector and recover money for damages up to $500,000, or one percent of the collector's net worth, whichever is less.

Report It

As we have discussed in this chapter, you need to know your rights. Report any problems you have with a debt collector to your state Attorney General's office (go to the naag.org website and click on your state's listing), and the Consumer Financial Protection Bureau (CFPB) at consumerfinance.gov. The CFBP has the authority to enforce the FDCPA. While government agencies don't usually get involved in individual disputes, they may take action against a collection company when they see a pattern of violations. Speak up!

Part Three

Great Credit

Introduction

When Robert Kiyosaki failed an English class in high school, his Rich Dad reminded him that his banker had never asked for his report card. His point wasn't that education is not important, but that your grades in school won't determine how much wealth you build over your lifetime.

There is a report card, though, that's much more important to your financial life than one you receive in school. And that's your credit report. Instead of "A"s or "D"s, your grade on that credit report will be a number: your credit score.

Your credit reports and scores play a strong role in:

- How much you pay for credit cards, mortgages, auto loans, and even some business loans.
- Whether you're able to borrow (hopefully for good debt) when you need to.
- The rates you pay for your auto or homeowner's insurance.
- How easy it is to get utility services, cell phone accounts, and many other services.

In this chapter and the next two, I am going to explain how credit reports and credit scores work, your rights, and most importantly how to maximize your credit to get the best deals.

If you have "bad" credit, don't get discouraged. Credit winners won't use bad credit as an excuse to avoid moving forward with their wealth building efforts, and neither should you. You can get to work improving it as soon as you've read this book. In the meantime, you may just have to be a little more creative.

If you want to buy real estate, for example, you can look for "hard money" loans, where the value of the property is what matters, not your credit. If you are starting a business, you can search out partners or shoestring it while you improve your credit. In other words, work on your credit, but don't let your credit stop you from reaching your goals.

Also, think for yourself, and don't be swayed by fair-weather friends...

When Charity Borders Insanity

Donna was everyone's friend. She was the one who could be counted on to help a friend in need, be it moving into a new place, a late-night trip to the emergency room, or lending a few dollars here and there until payday.

Donna valued her circle of friends. They were very important to her. She wasn't married and didn't have any family in the area. She enjoyed their company and believed that they enjoyed hers.

Donna did the books for a painting contractor. She was saving every month towards buying a house. She wanted her own cozy little home in the worst way. She wasn't sure she would ever get married and wanted at least the security of a place to call her own.

Then Lars came to work in the business. He was a tall, distinguished-looking man in his late 40's. He was hired as a business development executive for the contractor owners, who wanted to line up more jobs with government agencies and larger businesses. Lars was a good salesman and he took a liking to Donna. She enjoyed the attention.

One evening over dinner, Lars asked Donna if he could discuss a car problem he was having. Always ready to lend an ear and help wherever needed, Donna insisted that he discuss the problem.

Lars explained that he was looking to purchase a new Dodge Durango. It would help him in the business, but he was stuck on the financing. His ex-wife had run up a large number of bills on a joint credit card and the credit card company was coming after him for her shopping sprees. In order to finance the car he needed to have a co-signer involved, due to his suddenly poor credit score. Lars wondered whom Donna might suggest.

Ever the friend, Donna indicated that she could co-sign. She did the books and knew how much Lars was earning. There could never be a problem with him paying a $300-per-month car payment.

Lars insisted that he was not asking Donna to sign, he was merely inquiring as to whom she thought he should ask to co-sign. Donna then insisted that Lars look no further. She thought she should co-sign. She was willing to help Lars because she trusted him and she prided herself for helping her friends in need.

Lars was very appreciative. The next day after work they went to the dealership and signed the papers for the new Dodge Durango. As Donna was sitting down to sign, the credit manager asked her if she understood the consequences of what she was signing. He explained that if Lars didn't make the payments for any reason Donna would become responsible for them. Donna acknowledged this as she co-signed for the Durango. She knew Lars' character and income. There wouldn't be a problem.

Lars drove the truck off the lot. Donna followed in her car. They went to the nicest restaurant in town to celebrate. When Lars tried to pay for the meal on his credit card, it was rejected. He grumbled again at his ex-wife's profligate ways as Donna paid for dinner.

In the next few weeks Lars seemed to drift away from Donna. He wasn't as attentive or flirtatious. She thought it was due to the increased pressures of the job. With the new Durango, he was probably making a better impression and thus was even busier. Donna didn't worry about it too much, although she did miss the attention.

Then, one Monday, Lars failed to come to work. Everyone thought he was sick. One of the painters joked that he probably had the "bourbon flu," since he had seen Lars drinking heavily on Saturday night.

Tuesday, Wednesday … still no Lars. No calls to him were answered, so on Thursday one of the owners went over to Lars' apartment. The manager said he had cleared out late Saturday night without notice. Monies were owed, and if Lars was found the building manager wanted notice of his whereabouts. On Friday, Donna got a call from the auto-finance company.

Lars had missed his first payment on the Durango. They wanted her to cover it the next day.

Donna was shocked and dismayed. She had tried to help a friend. How could this happen? She made the first payment, hoping that Lars would turn up or call, or somehow take responsibility for the remaining payments.

Two months and two payments later, Donna got her answer. The Durango was found, totaled, in a ditch, a thousand miles away. Lars was in jail for driving under the influence and for vehicular manslaughter. He claimed he didn't remember a thing.

Lars had also let his insurance lapse. He had no money. Pursuant to the co-signed agreement, the auto-finance company sought payment for the entire vehicle and other costs from Donna. They demanded tens of thousands of dollars from her immediately.

Donna had to go deep into debt to pay off the Durango. In all, she lost her nest egg and savings for her long-awaited home purchase. Her credit score was so negatively affected she had to put off buying a home for what seemed like an eternity.

All for helping a friend.

Now, it's time for your credit report...

Chapter Thirteen

Credit Reports
Your Lifelong Report Card

Whether you're a real estate investor, business owner, or just a consumer who has paid bills, you've got a credit report. And that report is probably more important to your financial life than any report card you ever received in school. In fact, it plays a key role in what kind of credit you get and how much you pay. Even if you don't ever borrow or use a credit card, it likely affects how much you pay for your auto and homeowner insurance. So you have to know what's in your credit report, as well as how credit reports work.

Credit reporting agencies (more commonly called "credit bureaus") are in the business of compiling information about people's bill-paying habits and selling that information to other companies that may want to extend credit, insurance, or even a job offer, to them.

There are three major, national credit reporting agencies in the United States: Equifax, Experian (formerly TRW), and TransUnion. Plus there are hundreds of smaller credit bureaus that are affiliated with one or more of these "Big Three." These specialized agencies get information from one or more of the three major bureaus and may supply additional credit information as well. (See the end of this chapter for more information on other consumer reporting agencies.)

There are also business credit bureaus; Cortera, D&B, Equifax and Experian are the main ones that compile reports solely on businesses around the world. For more information on business credit reports, see the Resources section. Our focus here is on personal credit, though it can be valuable if your goal is to build business credit as well.

Credit reporting is big business, and the major credit reporting agencies are businesses in competition with each other. They are all trying to make their reports "better" than the others and they will not share information unless they are required to do so by law. That's one reason why, when you see your credit report, you'll see that it looks somewhat different depending on which agency supplied it. While most of the accounts will likely show similar information, they won't all be exactly the same.

Credit reporting agencies are regulated under the Federal Fair Credit Reporting Act (FCRA), which was updated in 1999 and again at the end of December 2003. You'll learn more about your rights under that law shortly.

Starting Out

Margery and Sharon were college roommates. They attended a large, Midwestern university – but that was where the similarities ended. Margery was prudent, studious and focused. Sharon was a party girl, living for the moment and enjoying every one of them.

While Margery thought nothing of studying on a Saturday night if her courses so required, Sharon was out all Saturday night and into Sunday morning. There was friction when Sharon brought friends over to their small house off-campus to finish off the night. Margery needed her sleep and let Sharon know about it.

Not surprisingly, Margery and Sharon were also different in their spending habits. Margery had saved to attend college and was fortunate enough to get a partial scholarship to help defray the costs. She did not want to burden her parents and was proud that she had not asked them for money. Margery did not want to incur a great deal of debt and avoided obtaining a credit card, being instead cautious and prudent in her spending.

Sharon, on the other hand, was anything but prudent. She lived off student loans, her parents' money and in the last year, three high-interest credit cards. Since they were recently maxxed out, she told Margery that she would have to get another one to help with next month's rent. Margery asked how she could handle all of the high-interest payments. Sharon explained that working at "The Rat," the local rathskeller and college hangout, on the prime party nights of Thursday and Friday provided enough tip money to make the monthly payments. The principal payments, like her student loans, she'd worry about later.

Margery privately worried that Sharon was headed for trouble. She was again thankful of her resolve to avoid credit cards and credit problems.

Soon graduation arrived and both of them found decent starting jobs in Chicago. They agreed not to be roommates, both acknowledging that their lifestyles were a bit too different, but did agree to keep in touch.

Margery soon ran into difficulty finding an apartment. When the management companies did a check of her credit, she didn't turn up. While there wasn't any negative information, there also wasn't any positive information either on which to base a decision. She had no credit history, which, as Margery soon learned, was negative.

Sharon called and invited Margery over to, of course, a party at her new apartment. Margery was pleased to be included with her old group of friends and, even more so, was curious about how Sharon, with her negative credit, had found an apartment so quickly. Arriving, she found that Sharon had moved into a spacious one-bedroom apartment with a large balcony and an excellent view. Greeting Sharon, Margery couldn't help but ask how she lined up such a great apartment. Sharon replied that the manager said she had credit because she made all of her credit card payments on time.

Margery woke up the next morning realizing she had to get a credit card. If four cards worked for Sharon, at least one card would work for her. She called a bank to begin the process. The bank checked her credit and politely declined her. Margery was getting frustrated and wanted to know why she was declined, especially since she had been sent hundreds of credit card solicitations during college. The representative explained that college students were of a different credit class. She was out of college, with no prior credit history, and thus, according to their standards, not entitled to a credit card.

Margery was at her wits end. Was there anything she could do, she asked the representative. Yes, came the reply. A credit card, secured by a $2,500 deposit, could be obtained. It worked just like a credit card, the representative brightly noted.

Margery was close to tears. She needed all of her extra cash for a security deposit on an apartment. She couldn't waste it on a credit card, no matter how much she needed to build credit. Margery hung up and, swallowing her pride, called home.

Margery's father flew to Chicago the next weekend. Together they found a nice, affordable apartment, which he – with his established credit – cosigned. Calling around, they found a secured credit card with only a $500 deposit requirement. If a good payment history was established over a one-year period, the deposit would be returned and it would be unsecured. Margery's father encouraged her to charge her groceries on the card and pay the resulting monthly bill promptly, thus establishing a payment history for some computer somewhere to latch onto.

Margery thanked her father and promised not to burden him. He said he was genuinely pleased that she called for his help.

Margery set about getting her apartment ready. When she called the power company to establish an account, they did a credit check. Now a credit warrior, Margery knew the response before it was given. Sure enough, due to a lack of credit history, a $300 deposit was required.

Margery now had to laugh at the absurdity of it all. She called Sharon to tell her about the new apartment. Amid the conversation, Margery asked if Sharon had to pay a deposit to the power company. No, replied Sharon, a deposit was waived for good credit.

You first build a credit report when you fill out a credit application and the company orders a credit report on you. If there is no information in their databases, they will store your basic identifying information -- name, address and social security number. Once you do get a loan that is reported, that information will then be sent to one or more of the major reporting agencies to start your credit file.

How to Get Your Credit Reports

The Fair and Accurate Credit Transactions Act of 2003 (which updated the Federal Fair Credit Reporting Act), requires every major national credit bureau to give one consumer a free credit report per year. In addition, you can order a free copy of your report from bureaus that compile reports on:

(1) Medical records or payments;

(2) Residential or tenant history;

(3) Check writing history (such as Chexsystems or Telecheck);

(4) Employment history; or

(5) Insurance claims (such as CLUE).

You can get your free reports from each of the three major credit reporting agencies at AnnualCreditReport.com. In addition, you can get another free copy of your report when:

- You have been denied credit or other benefits, or have received notice of a change of your credit status in the last 60 days.
- You are unemployed, receiving welfare, or have been denied employment.
- You believe you are a victim of fraud. (Fraud victims get two free reports a year).
- You are notified that you did not qualify for the lender's best rate or terms based on information in your credit report.

If you are going to buy a home or car, invest in real estate, or make another major purchase, get your credit report immediately. It can sometimes take 60 days to clear up mistakes. If you are a real estate investor, it can pay to subscribe to a service that monitors your credit report each month.

Who Gets Your Report?

With all the sensitive information in credit reports, you'd think companies would need your permission, maybe even written permission, to get your credit report. Not so.

The Fair Credit Reporting Act allows companies to obtain a credit report for:

- Employment purposes (by a prospective or current employer). Here they do need your written permission first;
- Insurance underwriting purposes (including when your policy is up for renewal);
- Considering your application for credit, or to review or collect an existing credit account (this could include applying for cell phone service, for example);
- A legitimate business purposes in connection with a business transaction initiated by the consumer; and
- Per court order or in conjunction with certain requests involving child support.

While there are lots of sources for ordering your own credit report, it's harder to get credit reports on other people. If you want to purchase consumer credit reports, for example, on prospective renters for your properties, you can go through an agency that supplies credit reports for that purpose. It is illegal to get a report on say, your fiancé or your ex, without their permission, but it might not be terribly difficult to do either. (Don't do it, though. The penalties can be severe. I just want to point out that the system isn't fail-proof.)

What's In Your Report?

There are four kinds of information in your credit report: personal information, account information, public record information, and inquiries.

Personal information. This includes your:

- Full name including Jr., Sr., or I, II, III
- Address used when requesting your credit report
- Previous addresses
- Social security number
- Year or date of birth
- Current and former employer information
- Variations of your personal information on file, such as nicknames former names, different social security numbers, different addresses, etc.

While it helps to make sure all your information here is correct, some carries more weight than others. CRAs aren't known for keeping accurate employment information, for example, so don't sweat it too much if that's not up to date. (Although correcting it wouldn't be a bad idea either.) On the other hand, if there's a social security number that doesn't belong to you, you'll want to get that taken off as quickly as possible since it could indicate fraud.

Account information. This is a list of accounts (called "tradelines" in the industry) you currently have or have had in the past including:

- Account name and number
- Date opened, closed
- Monthly payment amount rounded off to the nearest dollar
- Monthly payment history, usually covering at least 24 months
- Current status of account (paid as agreed, 30 days late, etc.)

The types of accounts that normally appear on your credit report are:

- Credit cards, retail or department store cards, gas company cards
- Bank loans,
- Auto loans and leases
- Mortgages and home equity loans or lines
- Consumer finance company accounts

- Recreational vehicle loans
- Credit union credit cards or loans
- Student loans

Types of accounts that do not generally appear on your standard credit report:

- Rent-to-own accounts
- Checking account information
- Accounts with smaller institutions
- Rental payment history
- Utilities or cell phone accounts, unless sent to collections
- Medical bills, unless delinquent
- Child support, unless delinquent

Important: No law requires that lenders report to credit reporting agencies. Some report to only one or two bureaus, while others only report if you fall behind. There are also specialized bureaus for checking account information, which we'll describe later.

Ratings Codes

When you get your report, most of the information will likely be spelled out in plain English. But the codes that have been around for years are still sometimes used so it's helpful to know what they are.

Open Account (usually must be paid in full in 30, 60 or 90 days)	O
Revolving Account	R
Installment Account	I
Mortgage	M
Line of Credit	C

Numeric codes for current payment status:

Payment Status	Code
Not rated, too new to rate, or not used	00
Paid as agreed	01
Paid 30 days late, or not more than one payment past due	02
Paid 60 days late, or two payments past due	03
Paid 90 days late, or three payments past due	04
Paid 120 days late	05
Making regular payments under a wage earner bankruptcy plan or credit counseling plan	07
Repossession	08
Voluntary Repossession	8A
Legal Repossession	8D
Payment to a Repossessed Account	8P
Repossession Redeemed	8R
Bad Debt; Charged off Account	09
Collection Account	9B
Payment to a charged off account	9P
Unrated	UR
Unclassified	UC
Rejected	RJ

You want as many on-time payments listed as possible.

Your payment history is the most important section of your report so you want to look at it carefully to make sure it's accurate. The sooner you spot mistakes, the more time you'll have to straighten them out (and it does take time). We'll explain how to do that in a later chapter.

Public record and collections information may include:
- Court judgments
- Federal, state and county liens, including tax liens
- Bankruptcy filings
- Collection accounts

Public record information is a little different in that there is no account number, credit limit or payment history. There's no rating, either, but these listings are considered negative.

There can be a lot of room for error here. One woman, for example, moved from California to Florida. A few years later she discovered the State of California determined she owed an extra $100 on her state income tax. But since they didn't have her current address, they had gone ahead and got a judgment against her. (By this time it was up to $400+ including penalties). She paid it off, but two years later the judgment had never been listed as satisfied on her credit report and created additional problems because it looked like she still owed it.

Collection accounts are another problem. Frequently, they are not listed when paid when they have been, or they are not listed in dispute when the consumer has legitimately disputed them.

By the way, in most states employers can review your credit reports as long as they get your written permission first. According to the National Consumer Law Center, many employers fail to give current or prospective employees the notices required when credit reports are used for employment purposes.

Inquiries

Inquiries list the companies that have seen your credit report in the past two years. It's not unusual to see companies you don't recognize in this section. First of all, companies don't need your written permission to access your credit file. They just need a legitimate credit, insurance or employment purpose. Requesting a new cell phone account could create an inquiry on your file, for example.

Also, the company actually accessing your report may have a different name. For example, you go into your local Dave's Flooring and apply for an account to buy new carpet for your home. That financing may be handled by XYZ Finance Co., which is what's listed on your credit report.

Warning: Inquiries from companies you don't recognize could be an early sign of credit fraud so don't hesitate to ask the CRA for more information and contact that company, if necessary, to find out why it reviewed your file.

As we discussed in the last chapter, only hard inquiries, or inquiries where you actually apply for credit, hurt your credit score.

How Long Can Information Be Reported?

If you have damaged credit, this is probably really important to you: How long can that bad information stay on your report?

The Long Shadow of Credit

Roberto had made some mistakes. He had taken some risks on a restaurant that didn't work out. The first twelve months after the business went under was tough. Roberto had been a sole proprietor and was personally responsible for every claim, whether he personally guaranteed them or not. Creditors hounded him night and day.

Robert's attorney had told him to incorporate to limit his liability. He thought his attorney just wanted to make an extra thousand dollars off of him. Now Roberto realized that spending the thousand dollars would have saved him tens of thousands of dollars in grief and lost sleep.

The restaurant supply company sued Roberto and won a judgment of $50,000. Because they alleged fraud and prevailed, Roberto couldn't dismiss the claim in bankruptcy. He paid $1,000 a month for five years to satisfy the judgment. His quality of life suffered greatly for those five years.

The other vendors – the produce company, the linen company, the landlord and the like, all threatened to sue. For six months Roberto had dealt with angry business owners. He had held them off by telling them the truth – he didn't have any money. Roberto was wiped out.

Then attack-dog collection agencies stepped in. The vendors had turned their claims over to some not very pleasant people who sneered hatred over the phone. These people, in violation of the law, called Roberto late at night and threatened all forms of damnation if he didn't pay off the debts.

For another six months Roberto had weathered these calls. He told the truth. He didn't have any money. The collection agencies threatened to sue. Roberto said that was their right. The collection agencies threatened to ruin Roberto's credit rating. Roberto said that it was already ruined.

Eventually Roberto developed a twisted philosophical – and useful – sense of the collection game. The collection agencies were paid to be nasty people, doing a nasty paying job. They had issues. While Roberto had failed once, he was still a moral person and thus superior in spirit to the venomous voices on the other side. He developed a calm in dealing with the collection agencies. The more they yelled and demanded, the more peaceful Roberto's responses became. The calmer he became, the more truly angry some of the collection agents got. Their vile and invective and voice levels became scary, even psychotic. But Roberto remained calm. He had learned that those who the Gods would destroy, they first make angry. By the end of some calls, Roberto worried that the collector would go straight home and kick the dog. But that wasn't his problem.

After a year, the calls from business owners and their collection agencies tapered off. Some had followed through on their threats to place a non-payment on his credit report. The report now read like an "F" in Money 101.

The last seven years had not been easy. Roberto had gone back to being a pastry chef. He worked hard for five years to settle the $50,000 debt from the lawsuit. His credit was so poor he couldn't begin to buy a house or a car, so he lived in a modest apartment and took the bus to work.

During the last two years, with the judgment now satisfied, Roberto's financial situation had improved. He was saving money to buy a car with cash. How he would pay for auto insurance he wasn't sure of, beyond providence taking care of him.

Then Roberto got another call. He knew from the sneering voice that it was from a bill collector. The voice demanded the linen company be paid $10,000 immediately or litigation would ensue. The voice claimed that the linen company would easily prevail in court, and, with interest penalties and attorney's fees, a total of $20,000 would be owed. Roberto remained calm. He asked a logical question. How long are these debts due? The collector became very angry. He shouted that the debts were due forever from deadbeats and that his credit report would show it into eternity. He told Roberto that he had 24 hours to decide between $10,000 or $20,000 and slammed down the phone.

Roberto had a sense that something wasn't quite right. He hadn't learned it in school – unfortunately school had taught him nothing about money – but it seemed that at some point a debt obligation ended. It seemed to Roberto that after a certain number of years he should be free of such claims.

Roberto decided to see his attorney for advice. He'd rather spend $200 than $10,000, if possible.

The attorney informed Roberto that there was a set period of time after which debt obligations expired. In legal jargon, this was called a "statute of limitations," or a time period by which something had to occur. These time periods, the attorney explained, have existed since the Roman Empire. Emperors were keenly aware that when enough time had passed claims needed to be extinguished. To allow disputes to continue for decades and generations was not good for the stability of the Empire. And so governments have continued with limitations to this day. While each state had a different time period for various matters, in Roberto's state the statute of limitations for collecting on a debt was seven years.

Roberto said that seven years had already passed. The attorney acknowledged that point and commented that the other time period of note was the seven and one-half years those debts could appear on his credit reports. That got Roberto's attention. He told his attorney the collection agent had said the debt would be reported forever.

The attorney laughed. He had dealt with liars for twenty years and no class of liar was more brazen than bill collectors who misrepresented that debts stayed on your credit report forever. The attorney informed Roberto that the debt fell off a credit report after seven years and six months from the date he first fell behind with the original creditor.

Roberto was now angry. The collection agent was trying to trick him into paying a debt that was outside of the statute of limitations, thus legally not owed, and was soon to be off his credit report. The lawyer nodded and commented that it happened all the time. Collection agencies would try to collect old debts through trickery. He pointed out that the Federal Trade Commission encouraged Americans to report such abuses at the ftc.gov website and presented a report about those complaints each year to Congress.

Roberto was only too happy to report them, if only to vent his fury. And, in another four months, his credit report was cleared of his restaurant venture. Roberto felt free once again, and looked forward to buying his first home.

Credit reports can cast a long shadow, so it is important to know how long information remains in your file. Here's what the Federal Fair Credit Reporting Act says:

- Bankruptcy: all personal bankruptcies can remain ten years from the filing date (not the discharge date, which is when the bankruptcy ends.) If you filed Chapter 13, however, and paid back some of your debts over a few years, then you can ask the CRAs to remove your bankruptcy seven years from the date of filing. In fact, in most cases they will do this automatically.

- Civil suits or civil judgments: Seven years from the date of entry (by the court), or the current governing statute of limitations, whichever is longer. Often credit bureaus will remove these seven years from the date of entry if they are paid.

- Paid tax liens: Once paid or satisfied, ask the IRS to have them removed. Otherwise, they are reported for seven years from the date satisfied or paid.

- Unpaid tax liens: Indefinitely until the lien is paid, unless you qualify to have them removed. We'll explain how later in this chapter.

- Collection or charge-off accounts: No longer than seven years and 180 days from the original date of delinquency.

- Late Payments: No longer than seven years.

- Delinquent Student Loans: If you bring a defaulted federally insured student loan current and make twelve consecutive on-time payments, and are not late for ANY reason, you can then request to have the previous late payments wiped out. Otherwise, seven years.

- Positive or neutral information may be reported indefinitely.

Seven Years From When?

This gets confusing. One consumer received an email from one of the largest credit reporting agencies saying that collection accounts would be reported for seven years from the date of last activity. But what does date of last activity mean? The last time a payment was made? The last time she used the account? The FCRA doesn't mention date of last activity, but you may hear it from time to time. Attorneys at the Federal Trade Commission have commented that date of last activity does not determine how long information can remain on your report.

The FCRA spells out very specific rules for how long collection or charged off accounts can be reported: 7 years and 180 days (roughly six months) from the date the payment was due leading up to the charge off or collection account. Note that it does not start when the account was placed for collection or from the date of last activity.

Example: Let's say you first fell behind on your January 2012 payment on your SkyHigh Bank credit card. You didn't make your payments so in June 2012, the bank charged off your account. In December 2012 it was sent to ToughTimes Collection Agency. That delinquency and collection account can remain on your report for seven years from January 2012 – the date the payment was due.

Collection agencies are required by law to report the original date of delinquency. If you can't tell what it is from your report, ask the credit reporting agency. If it's not there, dispute it. That's the only way they can tell how long to report those accounts.

Also, don't let collection agencies tell you they can report information forever. Those accounts fall off after seven and a half years whether you pay them or not. Collection agency threats to keep reporting negative information longer than permitted by law are illegal. If a collection agency tells you otherwise, report them to the Federal Trade Commission at the ftc.gov site and to the Consumer Financial Protection Bureau at the consumerfinance.gov site.

How to Get Tax Liens Removed

Tax liens hurt your credit scores tremendously. As I mentioned earlier, under the FCRA, tax liens may be reported indefinitely if they are unpaid, and then once you've paid (or settled them) they remain seven years from the date they were paid. That can keep them on your credit reports for a very long time!

However, under the "Fresh Start" program announced by the IRS in 2011, you can request to have a tax lien removed if you have paid it; or if you owe $25,000 or less and enter into an installment agreement to pay the tax and allow the IRS to take the monthly payments from your bank account. (There will be a probationary period of a few months to ensure you are making payments.) If you meet either of those qualifications, you'll submit Form 12277 requesting that the lien be withdrawn. It doesn't happen automatically, and even after you submit your request it can take a few months.

Other Consumer Reporting Agencies

Innovis

Innovis Data Solutions (found at innovis.com), when it's mentioned, is often referred to as a fourth credit bureau. It's not well known, and in fact it's very hard to find information about Innovis and what it does.

Currently it does not provide credit reports directly to lenders. Instead, it sells lists that credit card companies and other businesses can use for their marketing. For example, it sells a list of people who have moved recently, as well as a list of people who have been delinquent on their accounts (to be used as an additional screening for pre-approved credit card offers).

You're not going to be denied for credit based on your Innovis report. But you could be taken off lists for the most favorable offers so it's a good idea while you're checking your credit report to review your Innovis file as well. Instructions can be found at innovis.com.

Chexsystems, Telecheck and Certegy

Checked Out

Amber worked at a car dealership in the service department. She had worked herself up the ladder and had accepted a job as an assistant manager at another dealership five hundred miles away. She liked using local banks, feeling she received more personalized service at a smaller institution. So she closed her old bank account knowing she would open a new one at a smaller bank in her new town.

A problem occurred between the closing of Amber's old account and the opening of her new one.

Amber threw her old checks away, not in a shredder, but in an open trash can in the middle of the business office. Amber thought that with the account closed there was no need for any special precautions. She did not worry that someone in the payroll department had access to Amber's social security number, signature sample and, now, her checks.

When Amber was settled in her new town she went into a local bank to open up a new account. She was politely told by the new accounts representative that they would not be able to help her. Amber was confused and then angry. She demanded to know why they wouldn't open an account. She had good credit and never missed a payment. She was told she would receive a letter explaining why.

Amber left furious and went to a slightly larger bank. The response was the same – no new account – but the representative was more forthcoming. The bank used a consumer reporting agency, Chexsystems, that was reporting negative information about her. The representative warned her that there were two other agencies the bank had used in the past, Telecheck and Certegy, and that if even one company had a negative report it could make it difficult for her to open a new checking account.

Amber questioned how a negative report could arise. She had closed the account after the checks she had written were cleared. The banker asked her whether she had failed to cancel any automatic payments from that account that may have subsequently overdrafted the account. "No," she replied. Unable to provide her with any more information, the banker gave her the telephone numbers of the check reporting agencies. After a great deal of time and effort, Amber discovered that her discarded checks had been used fraudulently. It took her several months to straighten out the mess, and then get the negative information removed from her checking account consumer reports and open a new account.

Bounced checks or overdrafted checking accounts don't usually find their way onto a standard credit report. The one way these issues can show up is when a negative balance has been turned over to an outside collection agency. But your one NSF issue (non-sufficient funds) and returned check won't affect your FICO score.

That said, within the banking industry there are three agencies that do report such issues to banks and merchants which, of course, want to avoid bounced and fraudulent checks.

Telecheck maintains a database of bank and checking account information and then uses risk based metrics to alert merchants as to potential fraud before accepting a check. If you've ever paid by check and were given an electronic receipt of the transaction to sign you've seen Telecheck Electronic Check Acceptance˚ service at work.

Chexsystems collects information from member financial firms and then shares it back to them. Their reports help banks, and savings and loans and the like to determine whether a new account should be opened or not. This agency is where your NSF's and bounced checks will lead to a negative rating.

Certegy Check Systems, through their database and risk analytics software, also helps merchants decide whether to accept a check or not. If a merchant uses Certegy to decline your check the company has a service to help you avoid such problems in the future. It is called the Certegy Gold Application and it's free. By filling out the form at Askcertegy.com it can help you avoid most check declines.

All three services offer a free copy of your report every year. (Of course, if you aren't in their systems they won't have a report on you.) To obtain a free report contact:

- Chexsystems: 1-800-428-9623 or ConsumerDebit.com
- Certegy Check Systems, Inc.: 1-866-543-6315 or AskCertegy.com
- Telecheck/FirstData 1-800-366-2425 or FirstData.com

If you do have a report with one of these agencies, and there is a mistake, you can dispute it. These agencies are consumer reporting agencies covered by the FCRA.

If the information is accurate, and you still owe fees or charges to the financial institution that reported you, see if you can get the financial institution to agree to delete your report if you pay the balance due. Negative information will remain on file for five years and can make it difficult to open a new account elsewhere.

Watch out! Even if you never bounce checks, you could end up with a negative Chexsystems report. How? If you close an account and forget about recurring fees or preauthorized withdrawals, those charges could create an overdraft on your account that could trigger a report with one of these agencies.

Got A CLUE?

There is a consumer report may totally surprise you. It is a report not on you, but rather on the property that you buy. Known as the Comprehensive

Loss Underwriting Exchange, or CLUE, it is an insurance industry database that insurers use to deny coverage on problem properties.

Bad Dog, Bad House

Nicolas was ready to invest in residential real estate. He had overcome some financial hurdles and in the last year had purchased his first house. It was currently his primary residence, but Nicolas purchased it with an eye to turning it into a rental when he moved to a bigger house, as he knew he would.

For now, Nicolas was looking for another single-family home to buy to generate some monthly passive income. He knew his previous financial challenges could be finally conquered with an additional $200 a month in passive income. So, Nicolas needed to find the right property at the right price.

After several weeks of diligent searching, Nicolas came across a suitable candidate. It was a 3-bedroom, 2-bathroom fixer-upper house, with wood floors and a large back yard that seemed to be priced $20,000 under local market comparables. And the absentee owner was willing to carry an interest-only loan for two years so the new owner could get in and fix the place.

Nicolas was interested and toured the property. He noticed a sharp, pungent odor as he entered, but after a minute or two he grew accustomed to it. The property checked out and he made an offer on it with a $2,000 down payment.

In doing his due diligence and acquisition work, Nicolas contacted his insurance broker to work on covering the property. A day later the broker called back with bad news. He couldn't cover the property due to a negative CLUE report. Since Nicolas didn't have a clue what he meant, his broker explained. In the face of record claims, the insurance industry was targeting problem properties. If a number of burglary, water or storm damage or other claims had been filed against one property, insurers were now refusing coverage. The decision had nothing to do with the individual's credit rating, but rested solely on the property's prior claims history.

Nicolas asked what was wrong with the property. The broker explained that the owner had rented to families with dogs. Every time a family would move out the owner would submit an insurance claim for damage done by the dogs' expressions of territory. Nicolas noted the odor was pretty strong but asked why he couldn't get insurance if he agreed not to rent to dog owners anymore. The broker replied that future promises and fresh starts weren't a consideration. The property already had been marked by the insurance industry. They weren't going to go there anymore.

Nicolas appreciated the information. He backed out of the deal. Someone else would have to be clueless about the property.

It is important to note that only the current property owners can order a CLUE report choicetrust.com. As such, buyers will want to require sellers to provide them with an insurable CLUE report. Otherwise, when you can't obtain insurance on some real estate with problems, the property's negative profile may end up sullying your own good credit. There are challenges everywhere.

Now, its time to get scored...

Chapter Fourteen

Credit Scores

While your credit report is important, the numbers that are created from your credit report – your credit scores – may be even more important. Credit scores are mysterious and often misunderstood. But they're so important that it's worth taking the time to understand them.

How Much Is a Good Credit Score Worth?

Most people by now have heard of "FICO" scores. They're the scores created by the company formerly known as the Fair Isaac Company, and now just by the acronym FICO. FICO scores have been around for many years and they're the most widely used general type of scores. But you don't have a single FICO score because different FICO-based scores can be created depending on who is using them, and for what purpose.

There's one goal in creating a score, and that's to predict behavior. In most cases, lenders or insurance companies are using scores to predict the risk in lending money (or extending insurance) to a consumer. But they can also use scores to predict how profitable a current or prospective customer might be, to predict what will happen if you increase a customer's credit line or change the terms of an account etc.

Scores are created by analyzing the factors that different groups of consumers have in common. The goal is to find which factors those who pay their bills on time have in common, as well as the factors those who don't pay on time, share. Often FICO scores are based on information in the credit report, but they can also include information in an application or in customers' account histories.

On the plus side, there is simply no way credit would be as easily available as it is today if credit reports and scores didn't exist. If you need to borrow for emergencies – or for good debt – credit scoring makes it possible to get a loan very quickly. Credit scoring is objective, and for the most part, unbiased in the sense that they don't look at race, gender, neighborhood demographics, or other similar factors. As Gerri Detweiler has noted, there are some legitimate concerns that it is skewed against recent immigrants or minorities who may not have established a traditional credit file. Here are some basics to know about credit scoring:

- It all depends. Most of us think of credit scores as a "scorecard" – in other words, like a golf game where you tally up your strokes and see what your score is. But it's not so simple. In fact, there is tremendous data-crunching that goes into creating these systems. The most important thing to understand is that every factor is interdependent on the other data that's available. It's like a golf game where each stroke was based not only on the fact that you swing at the ball but also on wind factors, lighting and gallery noise.

  We tend to think of credit scores in direct terms...if I do X then my score will improve (or go up by) x number of points. With a score, though, the effect of an action like closing an account or paying off an account will depend on the other items in the file.

  Here's an example. You may have heard that each inquiry on your file drops your score by 3 or 5 points, or some other number. That may happen. But it might not. How much your score will drop – if at all – based on a new credit inquiry, depends on the type of inquiry as well as all the other factors in your individual credit report.

- Check logic at the door. While we often try to understand credit scores in logical terms such as "too many credit inquiries makes it look as though you're shopping for too much credit," the truth is it all comes down to numbers. Information in the score is evaluated to predict risk. If it helps do that, it will be included in the score. If not, it won't.

  Here's an example of this. FICO determined a few years ago that the fact that a person has been through credit counseling is not helpful in predicting future risk. So they no longer include it when calculating a score.

  I am not saying that credit scores are illogical, though it can seem that way. It just means that arguing with the explanations of why something is included (or not) is not that helpful.

  If you are turned down for credit or insurance (or charged more) based on a score, by law you are supposed to be given the top four reasons that contributed to your score. But even those can be confusing. If the reason is "too many retail accounts," for example, that begs the question "how many are too many?" There's no specific number that FICO can give you, however, since it all depends on the information in your file.

- You don't have one credit score. In fact, you have many different scores, depending on who compiled it, and when. If you've ever applied for a mortgage, for example, the lender likely ordered your credit report and score from a specialized credit bureau that could merge information from all three major credit bureaus.

  In doing so, they probably received a FICO-based score from each one of them. These scores were very likely all different – in some cases, quite a bit different. That's because the formulas are not exactly the same, nor is the information that goes into it. After all, a score can only be based on the information available. And since all three credit reporting agencies will likely have somewhat different information, as I'll explain in the next chapter, your score will be different with all three.

In the mortgage example, the lender probably took a look at the "middle" score of the three to help determine which program and/or rate you qualified for. In other cases, lenders may prefer to use a score from one particular credit reporting agency, or they may use different agencies for customers in different parts of the country.

- Scores are created when requested. You may think of your credit reports and scores as sitting in a file at the credit reporting agencies, sort of like a Word document that's updated periodically. But in fact, credit reports and scores are really only created when they are requested. When a lender (or you) makes a request for your credit information, the computers go to work gathering information available about you at that point in time, so that your report and/or scores can be created. That means that...

- Things change. New information is constantly being reported to the credit reporting agencies and so the next time your credit information is requested, your credit reports may change. The information reported about you may change a lot, or a little. And since your credit scores are based on the information in your credit reports, your scores can change too. If you file for bankruptcy, or if one of your accounts is turned over to a collection agency, your score can drop a lot. But it can also drop after what you think are positive changes, such as a bankruptcy or judgment falling off the report. This makes predicting what will happen if you make certain changes to your credit tough.

For example, John had a bankruptcy and two tax liens drop off his credit report after seven years. He thought his score would shoot up but it went down instead. The reason was likely that before, he was in a "had a bankruptcy" group. Now he was just a consumer without much in the way of credit references.

- More may be better. If you've been through credit problems, you may think that avoiding credit is a good way to stay out of trouble and build better credit. But credit scoring systems must rely on the data in your report to predict how you'll handle credit in the future. If there's nothing recent to analyze, your score will suffer. Also, if you have nothing at all it is even harder to have a good credit score...

Self-Sufficient Sam

Sam was a rugged individual. He didn't like banks, credit card companies, political parties, trade unions, television networks, charitable crusaders or religious zealots. Sam especially didn't like power companies.

Sam just wanted to be left alone. He lived in a small cabin in the remote wilderness of eastern Idaho near the Grand Tetons. Sam had long hair, a long beard, and a short fuse. He cut wood all summer so he could keep warm all winter and he used a propane lamp at night so he wouldn't have to pay the infernal local power company. At harvest time, Sam preserved blueberries, apples and other fruits so he had food through the winter.

Sam made a barely sustainable living stuffing envelopes in his spare time, which time was limited due to all of the wood chopping and preserving of food. Sam was paid in cash, which was fine with him. While he didn't like the Federal Reserve Board (that issued the cash notes), he liked banks even less. He didn't have a bank account, nor did Sam want one. He was a cash-and-carry kind of loner.

All of Sam's necessities were paid for with cash, and he was proud of the fact he did not have regular monthly bills. Sam felt his credit was excellent and superior to all others.

But Sam was worried about the health of his dear mother, who lived alone in Arkansas. He had often thought about calling her, but didn't have a phone at the cabin. The owner of the small gas station way down the hill wouldn't let Sam use the only pay phone in town due to some argument they had years ago about the evils of energy companies. So, Sam didn't get around to calling his beloved mother very often.

Then one day a U.S. Postal Service truck arrived. It was the first time one had ever come onto the property in five years. Sam didn't get any telephone or power or credit card bills. He didn't subscribe to any publications. And Sam certainly didn't get any junk mail. Five years ago, when the last postman had showed up to deliver a Publishers Clearinghouse award notice, Sam had run him off the property with what appeared to be a bazooka. Sam relished the fact that heavy firepower was still the only truly effective cure for junk mail.

The postman approached cautiously, with his hands up. He waved a white flag in one hand and held a white envelope up in the other hand. He stated that he had a letter for Sam from a family member in Arkansas. Sam told the postman to drop the letter where he stood and to slowly retreat. The postman did so and hurriedly drove off. Sam set down his bazooka and retrieved the letter.

It was from his brother, Elbert, notifying him that their mother had passed on. The letter urged him to come to the funeral. Enclosed was an airplane ticket.

Sam was ambivalent. He didn't want to see the rest of his soft on the grid family but he did want to honor his mother. So he packed up the old Studebaker pick-up and headed out early to the Idaho Falls airport for the flight.

Forty miles down the road, the Studebaker died. Sam got the old beast to a service station where the owner indicated that he would need a deposit to locate some very hard-to-find parts. He asked Sam for a credit card. Sam didn't have one, nor, as he belligerently noted, did he want one. The owner shrugged his shoulders. He would take cash. Sam forked over enough cash to satisfy the owner and saved enough for the cab fair to Idaho Falls.

At the airport check-in counter, Sam was asked for his identification. He showed his driver's license, which hadn't been renewed in three years. The counter agent asked to see another form of ID. Sam didn't have one – no credit cards, no store cards, nothing, and was defiantly proud that he didn't need such things – due to his excellent credit.

This situation rang off silent alarm bells with the counter agent. Angry, bearded men without current identification were not the airline industry's favorite customers. Sam was politely asked to wait while the airline did some checking. Sam growled that he'd better not be late for his mother's funeral.

In the back office the agent searched the national security database for Sam. He had a social security number with no real payments made to it. Otherwise he was invisible on the system, a unique and troubling prospect.

The station manager wondered how Sam had purchased the airline ticket. They searched and found Elbert's name. Searching Elbert's background they learned that he was with the Arkansas National Guard. They called for a confirmation. Elbert was eventually reached, and vouched that his challenging brother was, indeed, headed to his mother's funeral.

Sam was allowed to board the flight, never knowing that his excellent credit had almost cost him a seat.

Arriving in Little Rock, Arkansas, Sam realized that he didn't have enough cash for a cab ride to Botkinburg, where the funeral was being held. He thought it would be cheaper to rent a car. At the first counter he was asked for a credit card. Once again, Sam defiantly noted that he didn't have one, or want one. He was politely informed that without one, he couldn't rent a car.

Sam stormed off to the next counter, and the next counter and the next counter. He angrily fumed why someone with excellent credit could not rent a car in America without a credit card! A nice man in his mid-30's approached Sam. He shared Sam's frustrations and offered to help. He was headed up Highway 65 and could give Sam a lift so he could attend his mother's funeral. Arriving in time for the service, Sam thanked his driver. The man said no thanks were necessary. He was heading north on business anyway, noting that if anyone should be thanked it was his employer, the local power company.

As Sam's case illustrates, it is very difficult in today's society to maintain excellent credit, much less move about, without a credit history. You can choose to be a recluse in the mountains, but that is an option for very few. The rest of us have to be concerned about our credit profiles and our credit scores.

Currently you are better off having a number of credit successes. Generally speaking, four or five different types of accounts paid on time over time will make for a stronger score than if you only have one. Include a major credit card in that mix, and perhaps a car loan, mortgage, retail card and another type of loan.

This doesn't mean you should open a bunch of accounts at once. Doing so can also have a negative effect on your credit in the short term. But if your credit history is skimpy and your score reflects that, you may want to add some positive references.

What's In A Credit Score?

With a FICO based score, the higher the number, the better your score. Scores above 720 are usually considered excellent (850 is usually tops), those in the 680 – 720 range are still quite good, while those in the 650 – 680 range aren't terrible, but will carry higher rates. Once you start getting below 650 you may have some trouble getting credit or be charged high rates. These are general rules of thumb, though, since every lender has different criteria.

According to FICO, five categories of information (along with their relative weightings) go into your credit score:

Payment history	35%
Amounts you owe	30%
Length of credit history	15%
New credit	10%
Type of credit in use	10%

It's obvious that your payment history is the most important factor in your score. But there are some finer points here that you may not be aware of:

Most lenders don't report you as late to the credit bureaus until you fall behind by 30 days. (But they will often charge you a hefty late fee if you are just one hour late with your payment.) This isn't a hard-and-fast rule so always be sure to double check if you're having trouble meeting the due date. Sometimes lenders will close your account or up your rate if you are chronically late, even by just a few days.

Recent late payments, even for small amounts, hurt your credit score significantly.

Late payments will generally remain for seven years, even if you catch up on the account or pay off the bill. See the next chapter for details.

All other things being equal, how far you fell behind is more important than the amount. For example, missing a $20 minimum payment for 4 months in a row will probably impact your score more than missing a $300 car payment one time.

Account balances, however, play more of a role in a score than most people realize. It's not uncommon to hear, "I have excellent credit" from a consumer who has paid on time but has a ton of debt – and whose score is suffering as a result. There are several factors that will come into play in this evaluation:

How close you are to your limits on your revolving accounts such as credit card and lines of credit. The closer you are to your limits, the worse it can be for the score.

How much you owe on your total revolving lines of credit. Total up all your available revolving lines of credit and then total your outstanding balances. Ideally you want to use less than 10% of your available credit. If you use more of your available credit on your revolving accounts, your score can start to suffer.

How much you owe compared to other consumers across the country.

You don't have to carry debt to build credit. You do need credit cards as credit references, but you don't have to carry balances on them. You can use the cards you have for things you'd normally buy, pay them off in full and avoid bad debt.

The obvious advice is to try to keep your balances, especially on your revolving debt like credit cards (which is often bad debt anyway) down. But there's also another piece of advice that goes along with this: Be very cautious about closing old accounts.

Closing Accounts

If you've had credit for a while, you'll almost always find old accounts you don't use anymore listed as still open on your credit report. Unless you actually tell the lender you want to close your credit cards, they probably won't. (They'd love it if you'd use them again.) But if you do ask, they have to list them as closed at your request.

But is this best for your credit? Maybe not. FICO has said that closing old accounts can never help your credit score and can only hurt it. If you talk with a savvy mortgage broker, however, you'll hear how they had a client who closed some inactive accounts and boosted her credit score. But it can hurt your credit score, for three reasons:

You'll probably close the older accounts. While closing an account does not remove it from your credit history, once closed, those old account may drop off your credit history and this will shorten the average length of your credit history. With credit scores, a longer report is better.

I've already explained that credit scores look at your available credit to outstanding debt ratio. Close some accounts and you may appear closer to your total available credit limits. FICO scores don't care about how much total credit you have available, though individual lenders may take that into account.

Closing accounts may leave you with too few credit references.

Here's an email Gerri Detweiler, our contributing editor, received from a mortgage broker about his client's experiences with closing accounts:

> *I had an interesting day. First thing this morning I ran a credit report for one of my customers and got scores of 648, 677, and 684. She couldn't understand why her credit scores were so low since she ran her credit just two months ago and got all scores in the 700-710*

range. Since I couldn't see any reason at all why her score had gone down, no late payments and not a lot of other credit available, I asked her if she had closed any credit cards lately. It turned out that she had just closed what was most likely her oldest card. I don't see any other reason her credit took such a drop so this must have been the cause.

Gerri told this story to a colleague, who had a very different story. A couple months ago she ran her report and got scores around 570. She had 17 open credit cards and a lot of available credit but not one late payment. She closed 7 credit cards and was smart (or lucky) enough to close the new ones and keep the old ones. A month later her credit score went up to 640.

My guess is that in both cases the change in credit was so large because they are both very young and don't have a lot of credit history. I doubt that there would be so much of a change in either case if they had 20-30 years of credit but who knows?

As Gerri suggests, if you really want to close out those inactive accounts, do it one by one – perhaps no more than one every six months. FICO recommends you start by closing retail cards rather than major credit cards, and close more recent ones rather than older ones. Leave several open for emergencies as well as for a better credit history.

Inquiries

Whenever a company requests your credit report, an inquiry is created. There are two main types of inquiries: hard inquiries (which companies that request your credit report will see) and soft inquiries (which no one but you sees). Hard inquiries will affect your credit score while soft inquiries won't.

Soft inquiries include:
- Promotional inquiries: When your file is used for a prescreened (pre-approved) credit offer.
- Account review: When your lenders review your file.
- Consumer-initiated: When you order your own report.

- Inquiries from employers and insurance companies may be hard inquiries, but don't generally count in calculating your credit score.

Mortgage, student loan and auto-related inquiries

Shopping on the Internet for a mortgage or car loan can create lots of inquiries, something you need to be careful of. Also, when you go car shopping, it's not uncommon for the dealer to access your credit file. Sometimes they even do that without your permission or knowledge so watch out.

FICO has created a program to address this. All mortgage, auto or student loan-related inquiries within the most recent 30-day period (or 45-day period, depending on which version of the FICO scoring systems is being used) are ignored, while mortgage, student loan, or auto-related inquiries within a 14-day period (before the most recent 30-day period) are treated as a single inquiry. There is no special protection when it comes to shopping for credit cards or other types of loans.

Watch out: If mortgage or auto-related inquiries can't be identified as such, this buffer won't help. Also, if the lender is using older credit scoring software that doesn't incorporate these changes, it won't help.

Getting Your Credit Score

While you are entitled to a free copy if your credit report from the major credit reporting agencies once a year, you are only entitled to a free credit score if you are turned down for credit or insurance (or are charged more for it) due to information in your credit reports. The good news it that if you do receive this disclosure you will get the actual credit score that was used by the lender or insurer. The bad news? You get your score after the fact, when the best time to see it is before you apply for credit.

That's why it can also be helpful to find out where you stand once a year. In the next section, we'll explain how to conduct your own annual credit check up.

Credit-Based Insurance Scores

Some 95% of auto insurers, and 90% of homeowner insurance companies, use credit-based insurance scores to help decide if you'll get insurance, as well as the rate you'll pay. There is a lot of controversy around this issue. Some elderly drivers, for example, who had never filed claims, have been dropped by their auto insurers due to their low credit-based insurance scores. It's not that they had bad credit, they just never used credit much at all, so their scores were low.

No Credit is Bad Credit

Agnes and her husband Bill always worked hard and save their money. When they retired, they decided to travel, purchased a fifth wheel and started seeing the country. For the first time, they obtained a credit card just for emergencies on the road.

Their daughter watched their home and checked their mail while they were gone. They called her faithfully every Sunday from the road. One week their daughter reported they had received a letter from their insurance company indicating that while the insurance for their truck was being renewed, they did not qualify for the company's "excellent credit discount." Their daughter had already called the family's insurance agent and learned that even though their driving record was spotless, the insurance company was now relying on credit scores to rate drivers. Even though Agnes and Bill had never paid a bill late in their lives, their lack of recent credit references meant they did not get the best rate. The agent was going to find another policy but warned their daughter that credit scores were commonly used these days for insurance purposes.

In addition, there's always the issue of accuracy. If your credit report is inaccurate or you're a victim of fraud, that information can influence your scores. You may be paying more for insurance or other benefits and not know why.

Usually a credit score and credit-based insurance score will fall into similar categories. In other words, if you have a good credit score, you should have a good credit-based insurance score – but not always.

If you are denied insurance, or your rate is raised, in part due to a credit-based insurance score you must be told that and given information on how to contact the credit bureau that supplied your file to get a free copy. Insist on that – it's your right.

If you don't like the idea of your bill paying history being used to determine your insurance rates, the only thing you can do is complain to your elected officials at both the state and federal level. Then take my advice and start building better credit. Better credit usually means a better credit-based insurance score.

Warning: Some consumers have been taken by the "false credit score scam." A car dealership checks their credit. They are then told that their score is lower than it really is and given more expensive financing. Another alternative is for the dealership to use its own custom version of a FICO-based score, which turns out to be lower than the score with the bureaus. Your best self-defense? Always check your own credit scores before you shop for a loan, and apply for pre-approved financing with a lender before you start looking for a car. Be prepared for the fact that some unethical individuals misuse credit information and you have to watch out for yourself.

The Truth About FICO Scores

Following is a transcript of an interview from Talk Credit Radio with Gerri Detweiler. In it, Tom Quinn, a credit scoring expert dispels common myths about FICO scores. Tom Quinn worked at FICO for 15 years and his initial focus there was on creating and delivering credit score and credit-related educational initiatives at the time where the public was just starting to learn about credit scores. He later developed, launched and grew MyFICO.com, the company's consumer driven initiative to provide consumers with direct access to their FICO scores. He's a nationally-recognized authority on the inner workings of credit scoring models.

Gerri: Tom, I want to play a little game here. I want to talk "Fact or Fiction" when it comes to credit scores. We see so much information out there, and a lot of times it's wrong, it may be incomplete, or it may just be misleading. So I'm going to throw some statements at you that I've seen and then I want you to tell me whether they're fact or fiction. Are you game for that?

Tom: *Sure, sounds like fun.*

Gerri: Ok. So the first one is – fact or fiction? Every time a person applies for credit it costs them 5 points off their credit scores. True or false?

Tom: *That is false.*

Gerri: So what's the truth about it?

Tom: *Basically, whenever a lender touches your credit report or if you're seeking credit, then they usually will pull your credit report to understand your credit risk, and an inquiry is posted. So there are all these different kinds of inquiries out there.*

For example, if you come home today and have a pre-approved credit offer in the mailbox, a lender probably pulled your credit report to do that and then there's a certain code associated with it that can be identified as a promotional inquiry. Or, if you get a message on your credit card statement saying, "because of your great credit behavior we're raising your credit line," they probably pulled a credit report to do that as well and then an inquiry will be posted. If you go and try to pull your own credit report at myFICO.com for example, an inquiry is posted.

So the good news is, all those inquiries are tagged or identified separately so that the model can really isolate those credit inquiries that are related to you seeking credit than when you've actually applied for credit. When you apply for credit, what research shows is that people who applied for credit are riskier than people who haven't.

But the good news is, inquiries don't cost a whole lot of points in the big scheme of things. How you pay your bills and how you manage your debt is really what's counted in the score and so inquiries will add a little bit of predictive value on top and may result in a couple points lost here or there. But the way the inquiry logic works, a couple of things: Your inquiry is shown on your credit report for the last two years but that model's only looking at inquiries in the last 11 months. So those a little older than 12 months, for example, aren't counted.

And there's a capping logic. Basically, the way the model works is once you've reached a maximum number of inquiries for that particular score card, whether you have one more on top of that or 15 more on top of that, they don't count extra against the score. So, in the big scheme of things Gerri, inquiries get a lot of attention focused by consumers but they really don't cost that million points. Really focusing in on paying bills on time as well as managing your debt levels is really what's going to drive the score.

Gerri: Okay now, let me ask a related follow-up question to that, Tom, does it matter whether you're approved or not for that credit card? Just the fact that if they declined you, does that hurt your credit score?

Tom: *Well, the lender does not report to the credit reporting agency whether you were approved or not. The fact that a lender made a decision to deny your applications for credit, that denial activity or action is not reported so it would have no impact on someone's score.*

Gerri: Okay. So it doesn't matter if you were denied or approved. It's just the inquiry that could affect your credit score depending on the type of inquiry that it is.

Tom: *That's correct.*

Gerri: Let's get another question. Fact or fiction? A bankruptcy will haunt my credit scores forever. I hear this a lot, Tom, from people who are thinking about bankruptcy and they're terrified what it will do to their credit. Does it stay on there forever?

Tom: *The answer is false. The Fair Credit Reporting Act has rules and guidelines that the lenders and credit reporting agencies must follow regarding how long information stays on a credit report, especially information related to past due behavior, delinquencies, charge-offs and bankruptcies. And most information is required to be purged off of your credit report, negative information, after 7 years. The bureaus are very diligent about policing that.*

For bankruptcies, some are off after 7 years and some are off after 10 years, so there's a little bit of variation for bankruptcy. The reason bankruptcies cost so much on the credit score and result in a big loss of points is because they're extremely predictive. If you're building a model and you see profiles that have a bankruptcy on their credit report the likeliness of them having future delinquencies is very high. So that's why bankruptcies do result in a significant point loss. But they don't haunt you forever – that's the good news.

The score is forgiving and as that bankruptcy ages off of your profile, it has less impact on the score as long as your new information shows you're paying as agreed. And then, after 10 years, that bankruptcy will be deleted from your credit report and the score would never know it existed. Let's say, you've got a bankruptcy 11 years ago, it would never know it existed. It does fall off the credit report. It no longer has impact on the score.

Gerri: True or false? A short sale has less of an impact on my credit score than a foreclosure.

Tom: *Yeah Gerri, I'm hearing this question a lot or seeing a lot of misinformation out there about this and I don't know where it started. But the perception that a short sale has less impact on the score than a foreclosure is false. Actually, FICO recently published some information on some studies they've done to let the consumer* *population have a better understanding of the potential impact of a short sale or a foreclosure have on a credit score. And basically what their research has shown is that the amount of points lost for having a short sale or a foreclosure is about the same.*

Gerri: Well, so the take away that I hear is that the short sale versus the foreclosure, your credit score is not the main consideration there. There are other financial decisions you need to make, and it's certainly serious in either case, but it's not one versus the other in terms of preserving your credit score.

Tom: *Absolutely. Anybody who's making a decision about a short sale or a foreclosure needs to balance a lot of factors in that decision process. The credit score being one, but not the only one. But in terms of the credit score the impact of a foreclosure versus a short sale on the score is going to be about the same so that information should at least help them understand the impact on the score-related aspect of that decision process.*

Gerri: Here's one I've heard a lot over the years. True or false? Going to a credit counseling agency will hurt my credit scores.

Tom: *In general the exact answer is false, it does not hurt your credit score but it could impact your score depending on what action has taken place. So let me give you a little more background on that answer or it may seem a little bit ambiguous.*

Whenever you enter into a relationship with a credit counseling agency, the lender, if you're interacting with the lender, may report on your credit obligation when they report to the bureau. There's a code they can submit that says that you are in credit counseling services with that particular trade line or credit obligation.

The fact that you're engaged with consumer credit counseling services agencies in and of that itself will not impact the score. So the score does not look for that particular code and say, you know, this is negative, I should ding the score because he or she is with a counseling agency.

However, if in your interactions with that consumer credit counseling agency and their interaction with your lenders they are able to negotiate, for example, settlement of the debt, that can be different.

Let's say you, with a credit card, you owe $10,000 but through your interactions with that counseling agency you're able to get that card issuer to agree to accept $5,000 payment and close the account out versus the $10,000 you owe. Then the lender will normally report that the account had some type of partial payment settlement agreement or was not paid in full because you did not pay as originally agreed the full $10,000 owed. And that activity or that payment, that settlement indicator, would be considered negative by the score.

So that's why I considered it a little bit of a trick question because the fact that you go to credit counseling services will not hurt your score in of itself but the activity that comes out of that engagement, depending on what they are, could potentially impact your score, depending on, you know, the agreements that you reach with your debtors.

Gerri: Well, the other thing that I think is important to keep in mind Tom is that with many people going to credit counseling they have a lot of credit card debt and they're probably maxed out on some of their cards and that alone is hurting their credit scores. So paying down the debt and paying off that credit card debt could have a significant, positive effect. Correct? In terms of bringing down those balances on the credit cards?

Tom: *Yeah it's going to be case-specific, and if you have a profile of a consumer who has a lot of revolving debt that's probably already affecting their score and causing it to be lower. So let's say they reach an agreement with the credit card issuers to pay all that off, once they pay that off they will get incremental points obviously, for those characteristics in the model that are focused on the balances of the credit cards.*

But if they had no delinquency on their report and now all of a sudden there are these codes that say that they've accepted partial payment in agreements with the lender, they may be losing extra points for that negative information hitting the file for the first time. So it's hard to give a generalized answer on that since it's going to be case-specific in terms of the makeup on that consumer's credit report.

Gerri: Okay, and I'll add from my viewpoint. With the credit counseling program if you're entering into a debt management program, typically it's a full payment. You pay off the full balance over time and some interest depending on what's negotiated. Settlements usually come when you end up going into debt settlement or debt negotiation rather than just a standard debt management plan or DMP with a credit counseling agency. So there's a distinction there.

My advice to consumers: If the main goal is to get out of debt, get that monkey off your back and then focus on your credit scores. Don't let that stop you from getting the help that you need, if you need help.

Tom: *I agree 100%.*

Gerri: Tom, when we were talking about bankruptcy, you raised a little issue there that I don't think most people don't know about. I know this is getting a little technical but I'd like you to give an overview of it because I think it's important for people to understand, and that's the issue of different scorecards. That if I were to go and apply for credit and my neighbors were to go and apply for credit, and then someone down the street's applying for credit at the same exact bank, or we all go to Target and we all open a Target card, it could impact us differently because of the way the FICO system assigns people to different scorecards. Could you just give us a general overview what that means?

Tom: *Sure. We used to actually joke in FICO that the FICO score is more than a score, it's an equation and it's true. So there's probably this perception out there that there's one mammoth FICO scorecard that everybody gets scored on. But the way modeling works it actually tries to segment the population to meaningful groups or like groups of consumers based on credit information, so that it can optimize the credit predictiveness for likeness-oriented groups.*

To give you an example, if you have a typical family where you have the grandparents and then you have let's say a couple in their 30's who have children, and then you have someone just starting out, just getting out of college. Well, their credit needs and their behaviors are probably going to be very different so the older couple. The grandparents have probably have less need for credit or less active on their credit because they're in that part of their life where the house is paid off and they're not funding education, funding all these needs of the children so they have less credit, in general.

And then you can have a younger couple with children where there are a lot of needs, purchases and activities and etc., buying a house, car, cell phones, the whole nine yards so they're usually more credit active and using credit more fully.

And then on the other end of the spectrum, we have someone just coming out of college where they don't have a lot of established credit yet but they need the credit so they're out there seeking credit. So the way they model works is there's actually a system of scorecards and your profile when you're requesting credit will get sent to one of those scorecards based on whether the model sees any previous experience or delinquency.

So you'll be scored on what they call "scorecards" that will help specifically for consumer populations that have experience, and missed payment behavior in the past. And if you have no missed payments on your credit report, you may get sent to one of the other several scorecards based on how long you've had credit, missing credit, seeking activity (or debt) for credit, etc. What this allows is the model to do is to be more predictive and score you more fairly where you belong because it's scoring you in essence along with your cohorts against the entire population, and then that allows for a more robust model and a more predictive model which lenders value as they're making credit decisions.

All right, let's go from credit scores to fixing the ones in need of repair...

Chapter Fifteen

Credit Repair

If you're like most people, there's a good chance you'll find mistakes or problem items on your credit report. If you just have a couple of straightforward mistakes, it may be relatively easy to get them cleared up. If your problem is more complicated, or you don't have proof of your side of the story, it can take a lot longer. Some consumers have found it harder to deal with credit reporting agencies than with the IRS.

In Sickness and in Death

Carmen and Sean had excellent credit. That is until their lives were turned completely upside down.

Sean was a supervisor at the local branch of a nationally known auto parts store. Carmen was a stay at home mom who raised three great children, all of whom had gone to college and were now off on their own.

They were empty nesters and enjoying their time together. Then one day Carmen felt a lump in her breast. She was a little surprised but didn't act on it, thinking it may just be her imagination. Three weeks later she knew she wasn't imaging anything. Carmen's doctor confirmed it was breast cancer. An immediate mastectomy was required. They quickly obtained a second opinion from an alternative medicine clinic and just as quickly decided to stick with a traditional medicine solution. Before the couple knew what hit them they were dealing with surgery, radiation therapy, follow up visits and very large medical expenses.

It was at this point that Sean learned that the auto parts store had ceased providing dependent insurance coverage. Sean was shocked. Why hadn't he been notified?

The human resources assistant at the company's national headquarters said a notice had been sent out. Employees had the choice of having the cost of dependant coverage deducted from their paycheck or not. Many employees throughout the company had decided to find their own coverage for spouses and children. With over 40% of the employees deciding against paycheck withdrawals for dependent insurance coverage Sean's lack of a response wasn't unusual.

Sean was undone. He now had $40,000 in medical bills he thought were covered. He didn't know where to turn.

The hospital collection representative was calling Sean constantly. Carmen needed another $10,000 in treatments to battle the cancer into remission. The hospital needed to get the $50,000 paid now or they couldn't continue her life saving treatments. Sean felt very pressured. The hospital was very aggressive in their collection efforts he confided to a few friends. His friends agreed but could offer no solutions to the problem. Sean was desperate. He knew he couldn't tell Carmen about the insurance coverage problem. She was recovering slowly, but was fragile. Bad news could block her progress.

Sean did what he had to do. He started scraping together as much money possible the best he could. He liquidated the meager IRA account in a down stock market. After paying the penalties for early withdrawal of the money he had $4,000. The house had appreciated somewhat so he took out the maximum home equity line of credit he could in the amount of $20,000.

Sean still needed $26,000. The hospital collection representative was not really that pleased that he had provided them with almost half the money. Sean asked if there would be any more charges. The representative said he didn't think so. Sean asked if they would accept payments. But the payments they offered were far too high, and when Sean balked, the representative laughed and said they weren't a bank. He did suggest, however, that Sean look into a credit card that other people in his situation had used. It was a high interest, high fee card; it could provide him with $20,000 in credit right away.

Sean took down the name and number of the credit card company. Since the hospital collection representative was giving out advice Sean asked how he could come up with the remaining $6,000. The representative suggested that Sean avoid fully paying some regular bills for a while. Car payments, house payments could all be deferred for a time. Medical emergency was always a good excuse.

Sean knew that he had to get the money together somehow. Carmen's life depended on it.

The hospital recommended credit card was obtained and provided another $20,000 towards the medical bills. To the remaining $6,000 he would have to completely drain his savings and then stop paying some regular bills and apply the savings to paying off the hospital. Finally, in another two months the hospital was satisfied.

Sean's other creditors were not.

The mortgage company, the auto leasing company and all his other creditors were now demanding full payment. Sean explained his predicament and how the hospital demanded money up front to finish treating his wife and how the hospital said the other creditors would understand.

The other creditors did not understand and were angered. Medical expense emergencies were not an excuse to stop paying their bills. They demanded payment.

Sean had nowhere to turn. The high interest credit card payment and the home equity line of credit payments were both hitting him hard. He was unable to make full payment on either of them, much less his other monthly payments. He had paid the hospital to save Carmen's life, and was now losing the battle for a secure financial future.

Unable to pay creditors his credit report scores plummeted. The report showed numerous late payments, closed accounts for failure to pay, and accounts sent to collection.

Sean's only solace was that Carmen was recovering. The price was steep, but it was worth it.

As Carmen grew stronger Sean explained their situation. She of course understood, and, as with her medical condition, she vowed to recover financially.

Carmen and Sean began to live frugally, but such a lifestyle did not compensate for the larger debts they had. Their house, burdened by both a mortgage and a home equity line of credit payment, was in the process of foreclosure. Sean had learned of a strategy whereby an investor and/or renter could clear up and take over the house payments and share in the equity when the house sold. The advantage to Sean and Carmen was that by using such a strategy their credit report would not show a foreclosure. The disadvantage to a potential partner was that with the mortgage and the line of credit there was not a great deal of equity in the house.

But Sean vowed to overcome his condition and was persistent. He found a family who had been in financial straits several years earlier. They would not be able to obtain a home loan for several more years, but they could afford the mortgage and the equity line payments. Sean worked out a deal whereby they moved into the house and took over the payments. Sean and Carmen agreed to stay on the title until the new couple could qualify for a loan. At that point, Sean and Carmen would deed the house over, allowing their obligations to be paid and allowing the new couple any benefits of appreciation on the property.

Sean and Carmen moved into much smaller quarters, a one-bedroom apartment they could afford. It wasn't what they were used to, but the kids were gone, and the house cleaning chores were much reduced. Nevertheless, they vowed it was only a temporary move. They would be back in their own house in time.

Their Buick LaCrosse had been repossessed. That fact was a major detrimental item on his credit report. Of the 12 negative reports, the repossession of a car really stood out. Sean was a car guy and found a used car in great shape at a low price for getting around. That wasn't the problem. The problem was that if he didn't get the repossession off his report he'd never get a home loan again.

Sean decided to go right to the source. He called the credit department of the leasing company and started calmly negotiating. He questioned the amount received for the car at auction. He questioned all of the fees charged, from attorney's fees to repossession fees. (How could one repo man operating in the middle of the night ever hope to collect $175 an hour? If that was the rate, were they hiring?)

In a calm, reasoned and likable manner he worked on the credit representative day after day. He was never angry or belligerent. He was just the opposite. He developed a rapport with the representative, who started enjoying working with a kind voice on the other end of the phone for a change.

With all the extreme and various fees a total of $10,000 was supposedly owed to the car leasing company. Sean was willing to pay 20% of that if they would remove the negative information from his credit report. The credit representative had to state that 20¢ on the dollar was something that they couldn't do. Sean was undeterred and kept talking. He explained the situation with his wife and the hospital, not as an excuse or for sympathy but as a matter of conversation. The credit representative was incredulous. For a hospital to withhold medical services until complete payment was made, and to represent that medical expense emergencies were a legitimate excuse to avoid the payment of other debts was offensive. She said he would call Sean right back.

A moment later Sean had a settlement offer of 30¢ on the dollar. He accepted, relieved that a major negative was off his report.

Sean now had 11 negative statements on his credit report. He had learned that if he could get rid of at least half of them he could hope to once again qualify for a home loan. So he set about knocking them off.

The first negative report he went after was a department store payment he had missed. It was a small amount, only $189, but in the turmoil of scraping together $50,000 for the hospital the payment had been missed and now was on his report. With interest and penalties the change had ballooned to $375. Sean spoke to the credit representative, explained his situation and asked what they could do. The credit representative started out high but Sean got him down to the amount of $189, with an advance written promise to remove the ding from his report. Sean had learned that many collectors will say they'll remove the item, but once paid never do.

He learned it helps to have that promise in writing so you can force the issue later.

The next item to resolve was a fuel company credit card. He had only fallen behind by $215, but the account had been sent to collections. He called the collection agency representative to discuss the account, which with all the charges was now $289. The representative was rude, belligerent and caustic. Sean had to laugh saying that he sounded like a cliché. The representative grew even more nasty, which Sean calmly realized would happen no matter what was said. The representative was on commission and he would bully his way into payment however possible.

Sean discussed settling the account. The representative demanded full payment. Sean asked for a 30% discount and a written promise to remove the negative filing from his credit report. The representative laughed bitterly and said they didn't provide any such promise until the account was paid. Sean said that was unacceptable and asked to speak to the representative's supervisor. The representative shouted an obscenity and slammed down the phone.

Sean immediately called the fuel company to report the conversation. The fuel company's representative said that once the account was sent to collection it was out of their control. Sean knew that wasn't true and asked to speak to a supervisor. After waiting on hold for half of his lunch break Sean finally spoke to the supervisor. He explained that he was trying to pay off the account but that it did him no good unless he could have it all removed from his credit report. He explained that the collection company's representatives used obscenities, in violation of federal law.

Sean was calm and reasonable, which the supervisor appreciated. The account was pulled back from the collection company, a firm which the supervisor admitted was a source of problems. The fuel company promised to remove the negative credit filing upon a 70% payment. Sean paid the bill and another account was cleared.

Of the nine remaining negative filings four didn't really register with Sean. While things were hectic and blurred as he was trying to scrape together enough money for Carmen's treatment, he thought for sure he would remember all of the missed payments. But these four creditors, a stereo store, a medical clinic, a medical publisher and an equipment leasing company, were a mystery. Sean and Carmen had looked into alternative medical treatments but they had never committed to anything. Or so they thought.

Sean sent a letter to Experian, TransUnion and Equifax (much like the one found in the Resources section) disputing the four items he felt did not belong in his credit file. He knew that the credit reporting services and the creditors in question had 30 days to respond or the negative filing had to be removed.

As it turned out, only the finance company responded. After the information was confirmed as correct, Sean contacted the creditor directly and was reminded he had opened an instant credit account to buy a portable CD player for Carmen but didn't recall receiving a bill, and forgot about it. He discovered the address they had on file for him was wrong. Sean took care of the payment and closed the account. Given the mix-up and Sean's circumstances, the company agreed to remove the account from his credit reports.

The three medical related creditors never responded to the credit reporting agencies' requests for confirmation. This did not surprise Sean. The alternative medicine clinic they had visited had tried to pressure them into a series of expensive and dubious treatments. Sean and Carmen were immediately turned off and committed to nothing. Because those three creditors failed to respond to the credit bureaus request within 30 days the three negative (and possibly fraudulent) reports came off.

Sean now had five negatives on his report. Two were for credit cards he had been previously late on, but were now current. The new tenant (and future owner) of his house was paying one of them regularly as part of the house deal. Sean was paying his personal credit card on a regular basis. In time the late notices would become less important as he demonstrated a pattern of consistent timely payments.

The remaining three negatives were not to be cured. One was to the hospital for MRI charges of $7,000, another was to a radiologist to read the MRI for $5,000 and the third was for lab work of $3,000 incurred during Carmen's follow up visits. Sean vowed this $15,000 would never be paid. He had learned that the hospital should have never pressured him the way they did. They should have informed him that he had the right to go to another hospital for treatment instead of demanding every last nickel he had.

For these three negatives Sean decided to use a consumer statement. Under the Fair Credit Reporting Act, every American has the right to add a statement of up to 100 words to their credit report. It can be used to clarify or explain any items and appears on all subsequent reports requested by grantors of credit. Sean submitted the following consumer statement: "Our family suffered large, uninsured and unexpected medical expenses in 2012. Prior to that time we had always paid our creditors promptly. Since that time we have recovered and now pay all of our creditors promptly." While he knew his statements would not help his credit scores, he knew that if a lender reviewed his credit reports personally, they would see the statement. He hoped it would come in handy if he needed to hunt for a new job or get a mortgage.

Sean's good work at clearing his credit report and explaining his situation paid off. Within two years he qualified for a home loan. He and Carmen purchased a two-bedroom townhouse in a nice neighborhood populated with couples their age. They enjoyed their new house and appreciated everything about their new life.

How to File a Consumer Report Dispute

Picture the customer service department of a major credit reporting agency. It's large and it's busy. (It may even be based in India instead of the U.S.) It gets thousands of calls and letters each week. Some are legitimate disputes and some are generated with help from credit repair agencies, but it's sometimes hard to know which are which. Some letters from consumers are clear and easy to understand, while some are indecipherable, rambling and pages long.

Each complaint is handled by a customer service rep with one job: To keep the work moving. He or she will enter the dispute in the computer with a summary code of why the consumer is disputing the information. At the press of a button, that will be fired off to the creditor to be verified. The whole process of entering the dispute usually takes about one minute, and from there it's handled mainly by computer.

What does this mean for you? First of all, it means you shouldn't expect that someone is going to read the entire five-page long letter you've written about why the information in your report should be changed. It also means that you have to make sure your complaint will work for you and not against you. How do you do that?

As we have discussed, the law that governs credit bureaus is called the Federal Fair Credit Reporting Act. It gives you the right to dispute information on your credit report that is inaccurate or incomplete, and requires the lender or credit bureau receiving your dispute to investigate.

If you want to ask the credit bureau to investigate something that appears to be wrong on your credit report, you have the choice of either writing to or calling the credit bureau.

Calling can be faster – if you can get through to someone who can help you. If you call, make sure you take good notes about what was discussed, when and with whom. And before you call, make sure you can summarize your dispute clearly and in one or two sentences, just as you would if you were writing the bureau. Examples:

I never held this account.

This account was not late as listed.

This account was discharged in my bankruptcy and should list a
   zero balance.

Written correspondence takes a little longer but leaves a paper trail, which is one of the best ways to protect your rights. (Keep copies.) You'll also avoid getting dragged into a conversation where something you say be misinterpreted. Many credit repair experts advise you write, rather than call, but for a straightforward mistake or two you may just want to pick up the phone.

Gerri Detweiler advises you to write your letter by hand IF your handwriting is neat and legible. (Computer generated disputes can look like they came from a credit repair company, which credit reporting agencies don't like at all.) Date everything. Include your name, address, social security number and the credit report number if you have one.

Keep it simple. State exactly what's wrong, and what should be listed. Make sure that information stands out in your letter. (See our sample dispute letters for examples.) There's no need to use legal jargon or cite specific sections of the law. After all, the credit reporting agencies are very familiar with the FCRA.

If you have proof of your side of the story, include it. Never send originals, only copies. And only send documents that are really relevant. Trust me, no one is going to read your whole stack of paperwork.

Send your letters certified mail, return receipt requested and keep copies in your file. You should expect a reply within 30 days.

Don't bother filing a dispute with any of the major credit bureaus if you haven't recently ordered your report from that bureau, or from a company that supplies that bureau's report. For example, if you get your report from TransUnion and discover mistakes, you'll need to order your report from Equifax and Experian before you try to file disputes with them. They may not have the same information, and you'll need their correct contact information to make sure your dispute is handled promptly.

I can't emphasize enough how important it is to keep track of all your dealings with the credit bureaus. Create a file and note every phone call, and keep copies of all correspondence you send and receive.

The credit reporting agency usually has 30 days to investigate your dispute. If you provide information to back up your side of the story, they must share that with the furnisher (lender, court or collection agency, for example) that supplied that information.

The furnisher then must review the item and respond to the credit reporting agency, either by noting the item is correct as it's reported, or by making a correction. If the furnisher determines that the item is wrong, it must send a correction to all bureaus that have been given the wrong item.

If the item in question is incomplete, the CRA must update it. For example, if your report shows a charge-off but does not show that you paid it off, that information must be corrected upon your request.

When the credit reporting agency has completed its reinvestigation, it must supply you with a written response (either that the information is confirmed as correct, or that a change has been made) and must give you a free copy of your credit report reflecting any changes made. If no changes are made, you won't be given your report.

Important: If a correction is made, the CRA is not supposed to report the deleted item again unless the furnisher first verifies that the item is accurate and complete, and the CRA notifies you in writing before it reinserts if for a second time. This notice should include the name, address and phone number of the furnisher. Also note that you can ask the CRA to send a corrected report to anyone who received your incorrect report in the last two years for employment purposes, or in the last six months for any other reason. If you already were denied credit, insurance or employment based on mistakes in your report it may not help but it probably won't hurt.

Finally, be nice. Think about what it must be like to work at the credit bureau and handle calls and letters from upset consumers day in and day out. If you're on the phone and can't get anywhere with the person you are speaking with, ask for a supervisor. When you're writing your letter, at least be nice, even if you must be firm.

Don't give up!

Getting Answers

If you get your credit report and don't understand something on it, the FCRA gives you the right to contact the credit reporting agency to ask questions. It also requires each of the major CRA's to establish a toll-free telephone number, at which people who can answer questions are available during normal business hours. You're supposed to get this toll-free number with any credit report you order from the agencies. But that doesn't always work the way it should.

In fact, the major credit reporting agencies have had to pay fines totaling more than \$2.5 million as part of settlements negotiated by the Federal Trade Commission because they did not maintain toll-free telephone numbers with personnel who were accessible to consumers during normal business hours.

According to the FTC's complaints, Equifax, TransUnion and Experian blocked millions of calls from consumers who wanted to discuss the contents and possible errors in their credit reports and kept some of those consumers on hold for unreasonably long periods of time. If you have trouble reaching someone to discuss your credit report, it's a good idea to file a complaint with the FTC at the ftc.gov website. You can also file a complaint with the Consumer Financial Protection Bureau, which will be taking over the most enforcement of the Fair Debt Collection Practices Act. Visit ConsumerFinance.gov.

Credit Reporting Agency or Creditor?

Most people assume that if something is wrong on their credit report, they should notify the credit reporting agencies to make a correction. But that's not necessarily the case.

When the federal Fair Credit Reporting Act was first written in the 1970s no mention was made of the lenders (called "furnishers" in the Act) who reported information to credit bureaus. Trying to get them to correct mistakes then could be like pulling teeth – if you could get them to respond at all.

But in 2003, Congress amended the Fair Credit Reporting Act with the Fair and Accurate Credit Transactions Act of 2003. FACTA included more detailed requirements for companies that report information. It gives consumers the right to dispute mistakes directly with the lenders reporting them.

Here's how it works:

You have the right to dispute information directly with a furnisher (lender). If you dispute wrong information directly with the furnisher, it must notify the CRA's that the information is under dispute.

Put your dispute in writing and include any documentation you have to back up your side of the story. (If you can get someone on the phone who can help you, that's fine, but often all you'll have is a PO Box for an address.) The furnisher then has 30 days to get back to you with the results of its investigation.

The furnisher doesn't have to investigate if it determines your dispute is frivolous or irrelevant, or if it's substantially the same as one you've already submitted directly to the credit bureau. It also does not have to investigate if your dispute is initiated by a credit repair company. It does have to tell you why it won't investigate, however, and can't simply choose not to respond.

There are several advantages of filing a dispute directly with the furnisher:

1. It probably doesn't get as many disputes as the credit reporting agencies, and may have information in its files that back up your contention that it's wrong.

2. If it makes a correction, it will have to notify all the bureaus that have the mistake.

3. It's supposed to be careful not to report the same information again.

At the same time, the furnisher may not be as efficient as the credit reporting agency in handling disputes. If it's a collection agency, in particular, it may do a lousy job of investigating disputes. For some reason, collection agencies seem to assume that everyone who disputes a debt is just trying to wiggle out of it.

In the case of bankruptcy, a tax lien or a judgment, the furnisher will be a court and you'll have to find out which court has the information. This can be excruciatingly difficult, but stick with it. If the information is wrong, it shouldn't be reported anymore than any other wrong information. (The CRA should give you the name and contact information for the court reporting the information.)

The Big Problem

Here's what's likely to be the biggest problem with disputing information directly with the furnisher under the new law. The updated FCRA specifically says just the fact that a consumer says the information is wrong is not enough to give the furnisher reasonable cause to believe it's inaccurate. The fact of the matter is, however, consumers often find damaging information on their credit reports that they can't prove is wrong – they just know it is.

Example: Maria Rodriquez has a collection account from a major retailer on her credit report. She never opened an account with that store. She believes it probably belongs to someone else by the same name. But how can she prove it's not hers? So far, she's spent hours trying to unsuccessfully get the credit bureaus and creditors to remove it.

Dispute wrong information first with the credit reporting agencies. If that doesn't resolve it, dispute the item directly with the company reporting it.

Disputing Correct Information

There's no magic wand to clean your credit report if it's shot, but there are several things you can do if your credit report is correct but lousy. Here are your options:

Just Wait: As the information gets older, it becomes less important. As I explained in the last chapter, eventually it will all fall off your report. In addition, as information gets older, it carries less weight when your credit scores are calculated. Other things being equal, information in the past 24 months is the most important as far as your scores are concerned.

Rebuild Anyway: Take the first strategy of waiting a step further and start adding new positive references. This is important: It's not enough to get negative information off your report. You must have positive references to build new, good credit! Someone with no credit history (or a skimpy one) will have a low credit score, just like someone with a negative one.

If you have only one or two (or no) open available credit cards or loans, add some new references. See the section Building Credit later in this chapter.

Dispute It: Again, you can always try disputing negative information with the credit bureaus. If it can't be verified, it must be removed. This can be effective in the case of old debts where the furnisher may no longer have easy access to its records. Watch out, though, they may add it on again if it's later verified. (The CRA's are supposed to warn you first in writing before they put disputed and deleted information back on your reports, but it doesn't often happen.)

Ask for Forgiveness: One way to get accurate but negative information off your report is to ask the creditor to "re-age" the account. By "re-aging" the account the creditor agrees to remove the late payment(s).

This works best when the account has been paid on time for a good stretch but there were a few late payments with good explanations (illness, move, perhaps divorce). Don't bother to ask a creditor to re-age an account with lots of late payments over a long period of time unless you have a really good reason for it.

According to guidelines by the Federal Financial Institutions Examinations Council, creditors should not re-age accounts more than once a year, or twice in five years. The account should be at least nine months old, the borrower should show they are willing and able to pay, and they should make at least three payments in a row on time.

Your challenge will be finding someone who will actually help you at the lender's office, and then convincing them to do so. I recommend you be very patient and kind – after all, you are asking for a favor. But also be persistent. If one person can't help you, ask for a supervisor. If necessary, call back again. Remember what they say about the squeaky wheel.

Get Help: If you have multiple negative items, you may be tempted to try a credit repair company. Sometimes this can be a helpful route to go but be careful. Before you choose one, see our warnings later in this chapter.

Because an accurate credit report is so important, I want to review the rules here for disputes:

- Make your letter brief.
- Handwrite your letter when possible. (But only if your writing is clear and legible.)
- Keep records of all phone calls, if applicable.
- Keep copies of all correspondence.
- Send your letters certified mail or with delivery confirmation.
- Dispute inaccuracies with lenders first, then the credit reporting agencies.
- Be pleasant but persistent.

Getting Nowhere

What happens if you have a legitimate dispute and can't get anywhere with your dispute?

Example: Shana bought a car from a car dealer in what turned out to be a scam. As the investigation heated up, she stopped paying the loan on advice from the state attorney general's office, which even provided a letter stating that the information should not appear on her credit file. But her repeated calls and letters to the credit bureau got her nowhere.

Here are a few options:

1. **Complain to Regulators**. You can file a complaint with the FTC at ftc.gov and the Consumer Financial Protection Bureau at consumerfinance.gov. The FTC is supposed to forward your complaint to the credit reporting agencies involved and ask for a response.

2. **Hire an attorney**. Some attorneys specialize in suing creditors and credit reporting agencies. You can find one by going to NACA.net. If the attorney doesn't recommend a lawsuit, ask whether you can hire him or her to write a few letters for you.

3. **Add a statement to your file**. You're allowed a 100-word statement that describes your side of the story. While useful, note that the credit scores don't take those statements into account, and it's often your score that matters.

Building Credit

I've told you how important it is to build good credit. But if you have no credit, or damaged credit, it's tough to get started. Here are a couple of strategies that work well:

1. **Get a secured credit card:** A major credit card can be your best friend when it comes to your credit report – if you pay it on time. You can get a secured Visa or MasterCard by putting up a security deposit, usually $200 – $500 to start, with a company that offers the secured card. Use it just like any other major credit card and you'll build your credit. Just make sure it's reported to all three major credit bureaus or it won't be very useful. See the Resources section for more information.

2. **Borrow someone else's good credit.** If you live with a relative with a sterling credit history, they may be able to help you out here. Ask them not to cosign, but to add you on to their major credit card as an authorized user. You don't ever have to touch the card they'll send. In fact, its better you don't or you may be tempted to run up bills you can't pay.

If the issuer will report your authorized user status to the credit reporting agencies (and most will) it will appear along with the entire account history for that card. So suddenly, you can have a 10-year history of a major card paid on time. Just don't abuse the privilege. Don't use the card, and after you've built your credit history ask the person who helped you out to remove you. A warning: If they should pay late, your credit will be hurt.

Note: During the housing boom, credit repair firms exploited the authorized user trick and brokered authorized user slots on credit cards among totally unrelated users. Someone would "buy" their way into a better credit history in order to qualify for a mortgage. As a result, FICO changed its system to give these authorized user accounts less weight. However, using this strategy among family members residing at the same address may still be valuable, and as long as the new user doesn't run up debt on the card, or pay it late, it can't hurt.

Once you have these accounts under your belt for four to six months, then go ahead and get a retail credit card. After another four to six months, go ahead and add another credit reference. In another four to six months, add a third reference such as another major credit card or an auto loan. Your goal is to have four or five positive references always paid on time – and as little bad debt as possible!

You may not rebuild overnight, but you can see significant improvement in your score in as little as six – eighteen months if you stick with it.

Credit Repair Companies

You may have seen ads promising that you can get a brand new credit file, regardless of your past credit history. Or you may have seen warnings from consumer protection agencies that say that credit repair is a scam. The truth probably lies somewhere in between.

Credit repair agencies do generate lots of complaints to the Federal Trade Commission and other agencies that protect consumers. For example, when the FTC was more active, they filed 31 cases against credit repair firms as part of "Operation Eraser" – a federal-state crackdown on fraudulent credit repair companies. And a few years later, the FTC put over 180 Web sites on notice that their credit repair claims may violate state and federal laws.

Why do people fall victim to credit repair? The biggest reason is they are desperate to borrow again. Their credit has already been ruined and now they are looking for another way to borrow. Throwing your money away on credit repair so you can just get more bad debt is a lousy investment.

But another reason people want to repair their credit is that they've made mistakes and now they want to start building wealth. Access to credit at decent rates for good debt can help. That's a good reason to want to rebuild your credit, but it's not a reason to waste money on phony credit repair schemes.

Let's look at the truth about credit repair.

Myth #1:
We can show you how to get a brand new credit rating

These ads are typically touting one of several scams. One is to steal the identities of people who have died, sometimes in places like Puerto Rico or Guam, and use them to get credit. Authorities in Georgia, for example, uncovered a fraud ring that sold identities of deceased people for $500 – $600 apiece. The fraudsters scanned obituaries and then ordered background checks – including social security numbers and credit reports of the people who had died – over the Internet. Eighty people were suspected to be involved in the crime, in which they then used these recently deceased people as "cosigners" on auto loans.

Another variation is to offer to teach people to build a brand new credit identity. This scam is called "file segregation." One technique they teach is to get an Employer Identification Number, or EIN, which is similar in digits to a social security number. The idea then is to try to set up a whole new credit file under the EIN.

Here's what the FTC says about file segregation: "It is a federal crime to make any false statements on a loan or credit application. The credit repair company may advise you to do just that. It is a federal crime to misrepresent your Social Security number. It also is a federal crime to obtain an EIN from the IRS under false pretenses. Further, you could be charged with mail or wire fraud if you use the mail or the telephone to apply for credit and provide false information. Worse yet, file segregation likely would constitute civil fraud under many state laws."

But here's the real reason to just say no. It can be very difficult to effectively start a credit history – even with a new social security number or employer identification number. By the time you've gone to that much trouble you might as well have just worked on rebuilding your credit in legitimate ways. Save your money and do it the right way.

Myth #2:
We Can Get You Credit, Guaranteed

If you're having trouble getting credit, you may be drawn to companies that promise they can get you a major credit card or line of credit, guaranteed. The hitch is that they charge a fee, maybe just $100, or maybe as much as $1000 or more. Under the Telemarketing Sales Rule, if someone guarantees or suggests that there is a strong chance they can get or arrange a loan or other form of credit for you, it's against the law to ask you to pay – or accept payment – for their service until you get your loan or credit.

Here's another "guaranteed credit card" rip off. A credit card advertised heavily on the Internet promises an "$7500 Unsecured Platinum Credit Line." In small print below it, it says "for all kinds of our merchandise." This is a modern version of the "catalog cards" that were marketed in the late 1980's and early 1990s. You get a card and can use it to purchase merchandise out of that particular companies' catalog. Now maybe the merchandise is OK and not overpriced. (You can't tell because you don't see the catalog unless you sign up.) But even so, it costs $149 to sign up and you may have to make a hefty down payment on the merchandise you do buy.

Myth #3:
There's nothing that credit repair firms can do that you can't do on your own

While most credit repair is a rip-off, there are times when it can be helpful – if you find a decent credit repair agency to work with (a challenge in itself). If you have a lot of negative items due to a divorce, bankruptcy etc., or if you've been battling the credit bureaus or creditors with no success, you may need a company that has experience in working with those kinds of problems.

Just like you can do your own taxes or hire someone else to prepare them, there are times when it makes sense to hire a credit repair firm to take on the tedious task of correcting your file.

Unfortunately, the FCRA makes it so difficult to sue creditors or credit bureaus that most attorneys won't even take them on. There are law firms that specialize in credit repair, but some have gotten in trouble with the FTC so choose carefully.

You Have Rights

Credit repair companies are regulated by a federal law, and in many cases, state laws. Under the Federal Credit Repair Organizations Act, credit repair companies must give you a copy of the "Consumer Credit File Rights Under State and Federal Law" disclosure before you sign a contract. They also must give you a written contract that spells out your rights and obligations. Please read the contract.

You have specific protections under that law. For example, a credit repair company cannot:

- make false claims about their services;
- perform any services until they have your signature on a written contract and have completed a three-day waiting period. During this time, you can cancel the contract without paying any fees; or
- charge you until they have completed the promised services.

Many of the credit repair firms get around the upfront money clause by charging a fee for educational services, then performing the credit repair. Many will refund fees if they can't successfully remove items from your file.

Please be careful about spending your money on credit repair. There are so many rip-offs out there that it's important you check out any company carefully, and even then still consider what you can do on your own.

Now let's review some of the common problems associated with credit reports...

Chapter Sixteen

Common Credit Report Problems

Here are some of the common problems on credit reports that trip people up, along with some advise on what you can do about them.

Joint and Cosigned Accounts

You cosigned a credit card or loan for your boyfriend, coworker, or your ex. Now they've defaulted and you're stuck with the bad credit. If you agreed to the account when it was opened, it's accurate and you have to deal with it as accurate information (see below).

Example: Sara cosigned on a Visa card for her daughter when she went to college. Since her daughter always paid the bills on time, she forgot about it. Within several years, Sara's daughter had gotten married and was now getting divorced. In the meantime, she had also added her husband to the account. He ran up large bills and ran off without paying them. Sara's credit was trashed along with her daughter's.

If you've cosigned a credit card and don't want to be part of it anymore, at least get the account closed to new future charges. Don't let the creditor bully you into thinking you need the other person's consent to do that. (Sometimes they say they won't close it out without both parties' consent.) If necessary, get an attorney to write a letter stating you want the account closed and won't be responsible for any new charges. Doing this won't remove the account from your credit report, but could protect you from future debt.

Authorized Users

If you've ever asked your credit card issuer to send you a card for your spouse or child, you've requested an authorized user on your account. An authorized user is different than a joint account holder in that they don't sign for (or agree to) the account. So they are not legally responsible for the bills, but they are entitled to use the account. If you do add someone else to your account as an authorized user, you'll be stuck with any charges they make, so be careful.

If the authorized user is a spouse, The Equal Credit Opportunity Act requires lenders to report the account in both names to credit reporting agencies (provided the creditor reports accounts to one more CRA's.) Watch out if you have an authorized user (or are one) and are going through divorce, bankruptcy or other problems that can affect your credit. Get your name off the account quickly if you think they may have problems paying it on time.

If you were an authorized user on an account that went bad, ask the lender to remove the account from your credit history since you weren't responsible legally for it.

Divorce

Divorce can be tough enough without having to deal with the effects of a ruined credit rating. The most common scenario is that the judge assigns joint accounts to one spouse in the divorce decree. The other spouse figures they are off the hook. But the divorce decree does not erase the original contract with the creditor. Joint accounts can still be reported on your credit report – seven years for negative information and indefinitely for positive information.

Think about it. Most creditors would much rather have two people to collect from than one, so they are unwilling to remove a spouse from a cosigned account. But some consumers have been successful in persuading creditors to remove from their credit reports accounts that were assigned to their ex's in divorce. It doesn't hurt to try. The exception? If your ex is currently behind on one of the joint accounts, contacting the creditor or collection agency could mean they'll start coming after you.

Love, Money and Credit

Denny and Lyn were star-crossed lovers. Their friends all felt that the universe would have been a much better place if they had never met. Like a black hole, the two sucked all light and matter into a vortex of inescapable weight and gravity. And just as black holes aren't much fun for planets, Denny and Lyn weren't much fun for the friends and family in their orbit.

It all started out innocently enough. Denny was the star halfback at a small southern college. Lyn was the prettiest, most popular cheerleader. They were destined to at least date each other. Everyone would have been happier if it had stopped there. Why did they have to keep going together and eventually get married?

Denny was a prolific yard gainer for his Division II School but realized he didn't have the size to make it into the pros. It didn't matter. On top of his athletic ability, charm and good looks, Denny had a brain. He excelled in science and was admitted to medical school in the northwest. He breezed through the rigors of the training and found his calling, becoming a gynecologist.

Lyn followed Denny to the northwest. While he was studying day and night she had nothing to do. Lyn too, in addition to good looks and a winning manner, had a brain. She decided to continue her education while she waited for Denny to ask her to get married. She applied to the school's law school and was promptly accepted.

In what seemed like a flash Denny was a board certified gynecologist and Lyn was a licensed attorney. They were both attractive, well educated and polished: The perfect couple. It was inevitable they get married and soon they were Denny and Lyn, husband and wife.

Two children, a perfect boy and a perfect girl soon followed, as did larger houses and nicer cars. They were ever more successful in their respective fields.

Eventually, the mix of success and money, good looks and active synapses started to make for a destructive brew. Denny and Lyn could get whatever they wanted. Whether with their looks or their power or their money or all of them combined there were no restrictions on them. And with no restrictions the bounds of morality, humility and discretion that others felt did not apply. Denny and Lyn were free to take whatever they wanted.

Denny had always had a fair number of his numerous female patients attracted to him. Some were less subtle than others. He accepted that as part of the natural doctor-patient relationship. But then Laura, a former gymnast in her late 20's, came in for an initial check up. She was trim and sensuous.

There were immediate sparks between the two of them. Denny had experienced such strong attraction on two previous occasions with patients. But he was married with two children, he had told himself. He was also the doctor, and in a position of power. He had suppressed any feelings in the past.

Denny couldn't this time. The thrill wasn't as strong with Lyn. She was spending too many hours practicing law, and when they were together at home they were taking care of the children. There was no sizzle in their marriage.

A fling with Laura seemed perfectly natural. Laura was more than willing. Denny rationalized it might improve his marriage.

Lyn was spending a great deal of time at work. She had become a partner in the 300-attorney firm, a rising star in the commercial litigation department. One of the firm's biggest clients, a large food products company, had requested that Lyn handle all their litigation. Marshall, the president of the company was very attracted to Lyn. He enjoyed her company, and admired her physical presence.

A hearing on one of the company's litigation matters was being heard in a federal court across the country. Marshall and Lyn traveled on the corporate jet to the hearing. That night at dinner the two had a few too many glasses of wine. Inhibitions were loosened. Lyn felt a thrill with

Marshall that she didn't feel with Denny lately. A fling with Marshall seemed perfectly natural. Lyn rationalized it might improve her marriage.

And so events were put into motion.

Friends told friends who told more friends and soon everyone knew of the double infidelity.

Denny moved out. It didn't work out with Laura. She claimed he misused his position as a doctor. The state medical board was investigating this serious charge. Denny was undeterred and soon was seeing a parade of former patients.

Marshall's wife found out. Her family owned the food products company. This large and powerful client threatened to take their legal work elsewhere unless Lyn was fired by the firm.

Lyn was fired.

Denny and Lyn blamed each other for their sudden change in fortunes. A nasty and very public divorce ensued. Friends and family were forced to take sides. Friendships were lost over which side was chosen. The ripple effect of the divorce far exceeded the lives of the two parents and two children. It was destructive and unavoidable and left many good people wishing the two had never married.

When the bitter and expensive proceedings were all over the court split things roughly in half anyway. Lyn ended up with the house. Because their earning power was almost equal the court awarded Lyn with $5,000 a month in child support payments with Denny receiving weekend visitation rights.

Being fired by her firm made finding another job difficult for Lyn. She was now damaged goods in the rarified world of large law firms. She thought about going out on her own but was honestly tired of practicing law. After all the firm politics and client demands she needed a break. She recalled the old lawyer's joke that the best practice was one without clients. With the $5,000 a month she was getting from Denny she thought she could make the house payment and take care of the kids.

But she couldn't. Her expenses ran about $6,000 a month, especially now that she was dating her in home computer IT consultant who was in his early 30's and needed to be kept happy.

Lyn reasoned that Denny owed her even more money to take care of his children. She applied for a new joint credit card using both of their financial information. Of course, Lyn knew all of Denny's particulars. And because she wasn't working his employment history certainly helped secure the high limit credit card.

Lyn took care of the children but she also was having some fun. When Denny had the kids on the weekend she and the IT consultant would fly to San Francisco to shop or Reno to ski. They were enjoyable and expensive sojourns.

Soon Lyn fell behind on the house payments. She wasn't worried. Denny's attorney had forgot to address the issue during the nasty divorce. Her counsel had told her what she already knew as an attorney: If both parties remain responsible for the mortgage and the spouse awarded the house fails to make the monthly payments the other spouse is still responsible for the loan.

This fact hit Denny like a ton of bricks when he went out shopping for a new house.

After dating a full complement of ladies around town Denny had fallen for Jennifer, a young, recently divorced mother of two. They had a great deal in common, including incredibly contentions divorce proceedings in the recent past. Unlike Denny's situation, Jennifer's settlement required that the house be sold or refinanced. With Denny needing a place for his two children and now Jennifer's two children it made sense to locate a larger home together.

Denny and Jennifer found the perfect house for their combined four children. It had a big yard and a nice pool and it was ready to move into and enjoy.

Until Denny learned of his credit problems. Lyn hadn't made the house payment for three months now. It was in pre-foreclosure proceedings. Lyn also had failed to make the payments on the joint credit card she obtained without his knowledge for the last two months.

Denny's credit was in terrible shape. He was not going to be buying a house anytime soon. Jennifer was furious. Denny asked for her understanding. She had been through a nasty divorce too and he felt she should appreciate his situation. But she didn't. She needed a house for her children. She demanded that they get Denny's credit straightened our immediately.

Denny and Jennifer met with a local attorney specializing in credit issues. Denny first wanted to know if he could buy his old house in pre-foreclosure. It had appreciated greatly and if he could pick it up he could make some good money.

Jennifer bristled at the idea. She didn't want him anywhere near the old house.

Before Denny could get angry the attorney informed them because the house was several months behind in payments, the lender had called the entire balance due. If Denny wanted his house back, he needed to get his credit straightened out. The attorney stated that the first issue to be dealt with was the joint credit card that Lyn had taken out without Denny's permission. The attorney suggested the proper way to handle it was for Denny to file a police report on the fraudulent activity. It was only with a police report that the credit card company would investigate the matter and ultimately remove the negative credit scores from Denny's credit report.

Denny said he couldn't file a police report on Lyn. She was the mother of his children, and she took care of them 80% of the time. He wasn't going to have his children raised by a felon.

With this Jennifer blew. She threw down an ultimatum: It was either Lyn or her. Denny again asked for her understanding. But Jennifer got up and walked out of the office.

Denny and the attorney sat for a moment in stunned silence. When Denny started to laugh with relief, the attorney knew why and had to chuckle himself.

Together they worked out a plan to restore Denny's credit. It involved tapping into some of Denny's retirement plans, paying some penalties for early withdrawals and using the cash to get him clean. They paid off Lyn's credit card and shut the card down. The card issuer agreed to re-age the account and remove the late payments in exchange for Denny's full payment. They also arranged a work out agreement with the lender that brought the house payment current, then petitioned the court to require Lyn to sell or refinance it.

Lyn was shaken by these moves back into a mode of responsibility. Ditching the computer consultant, she found a low stress, reasonably paying job with a public interest legal group. She sold the expensive mansion she didn't really need and found a nice home in a decent neighborhood with good schools for the children.

Denny was able to straighten out his credit issues in a short period of time. He had the satisfaction of knowing he had avoided a second certain divorce and that his children would not be raised by a felon.

If you are separating it is essential that you:

1. Close joint accounts to further charges.
2. Stipulate that your ex will refinance the house or sell it within a certain time period, if you are both on the note.
3. Transfer any joint balances to individual accounts if at all possible.
4. Monitor your credit report monthly for fraud or future problems.

Marriage and Credit

Some financial experts advise showing each other your credit report before you say "I do." It's not bad advice. At a minimum, understand what marriage does to your credit. If you have separate credit together before you marry, there's no reason to join all of it.

Simply getting married won't merge your credit history. You'll have to add your new spouse to your accounts or vice versa for them to be reported on both your credit reports.

Example: Justin and Kayla are getting married. She has a few student loans, always paid on time, and just one credit card. He's already trashed his credit. If she adds him on to her accounts, she runs the risk that he'll run up bills that she'll be stuck with. If he adds her to his accounts, she'll instantly be saddled with those negative accounts on her credit history. A low limit joint account they open together may be their safest bet – if she wants to take that risk.

My advice is to maybe have one joint account you use for joint household purchases but keep the rest separate. Of course, your auto loans or mortgage may be joint debts, but they don't necessarily have to be. If one of you needs to build a better credit rating, you can try the strategy of "borrowing" their good credit that we describe under the section Building Credit.

Warning! Watch out in community property states (Arizona, California, Idaho, Louisiana, Nevada, New Mexico, Texas, Washington and Wisconsin) because in those states all debt incurred by each spouse during the marriage may become part of the community property – meaning you could get stuck with his or her bills. Even then, however, your individual accounts will not be reported on your spouse's credit report or vice versa.

Here's a problem Gerri Detweiler has seen come up when a spouse or ex-spouse files bankruptcy. Any joint accounts included in the bankruptcy may be listed on the credit report as included in bankruptcy. Due to a lawsuit a few years back, the credit bureaus have changed their system to search and find out whether the spouse who didn't file was involved in the bankruptcy. If not, the bureaus say they will not list the bankruptcy on the "innocent" spouse's credit report. But creditors may still do so if they are not careful.

Example: Kevin filed for bankruptcy but his wife Marta did not. They had a joint retail credit card that had not been used for some time and was not included in the bankruptcy. Because Kevin filed, however, the card issuer closed the account and reported it on both credit reports as "included in bankruptcy" even though it wasn't. Marta had to ask the card issuer to remove the bankruptcy from her credit report since it wasn't accurate.

Death and Debt

If you held joint accounts with someone who died, then you will be responsible for the bills. If you live in a community property state and your spouse dies, you may be responsible for all debt incurred during the marriage. But otherwise, you are not responsible for those bills. This includes parents whose children obtained their own credit cards without a parent cosigner, as well as adults who have been added to their parent's cards as authorized users so they could help them manage their finances.

The creditor may try to collect from the estate, if there is any. Whether they will do so depends on the size of the debt and whether it believes it can succeed. Don't be pressured into paying those bills directly, especially if it will hurt your family financially.

Credit card issuers will sometimes try to guilt or even trick children, spouses or parents into paying the individual bills of the deceased. As we discussed in Chapter Four in Elena's case, they may falsely tell the survivor that the debt is their responsibility. Or they will offer to "transfer" the balance to a new account in their name. In one appalling situation, a college student committed suicide after running up large debts, and the card issuers hounded his mother to pay those bills for the next couple of years. As we stated earlier, if you run into this situation, don't agree to anything until you contact an attorney. You may want to also consider complaining to the banking regulators and/or your state attorney general's office.

Mixed Up

You may find accounts you don't recall ever owning. It's possible that through a bank merger or the sale of some accounts, your account went to a new lender and you just don't recognize the name of the new lender. Or it's possible they have you mixed up with someone else – especially if you have a common name. Contact the creditor to clarify it. Worse case scenario, an account you don't recognize could signal identity theft.

Old Balances

The balance that's reported on an account is the balance reported on the day the creditor sends its data to the CRA's. If you pay off your account in full each month, your account may not show a zero balance unless it happens to be reported before you made new charges to the account. When you pay off an account completely, it can take up to 45 days or so to actually show up on your credit report.

Example: Richard travels internationally for business. He has an American Express card that he uses for those purposes. His monthly travel expenses are sometimes as high as $10,000 to $20,000, which he pays in full when he is reimbursed. His credit report shows high balances on those accounts even though he pays it in full.

If you have an account that was charged off, it may show a balance until it is paid or settled. A paid tax lien or collection account should show a zero balance. If you've paid off an account at least three months ago and the report still lists a balance, by all means dispute it.

Unauthorized Inquiries

It's difficult to get inquiries removed. The main reason is that the FCRA requires credit bureaus to show you the names of companies that have inquired into your credit for the last year (two years for employment inquiries). Even if a review of your report wasn't authorized, the fact remains that someone accessed your file and the bureau is supposed to tell you that.

If you have multiple unauthorized inquiries on your report – if you're a fraud victim in particular – you can ask the credit bureau to block those inquiries. If they are blocked, no one will see them but you and they won't affect your credit score. If you have a few inquiries you didn't expect, however, you'll have to decide if it's worth the time or trouble to try to dispute them.

Bankruptcy

When you file bankruptcy, the bankruptcy is listed, as well as each of the accounts included in bankruptcy. While bankruptcy can offer a "fresh start" from debts it does not wipe out the original accounts that appeared on your report. If an account was charged off in bankruptcy, for example, it may be listed as a "charge off," or "profit and loss" account, but it shouldn't show a balance if your bankruptcy is completed. If it does, dispute it and include a copy of your list of your discharged debts from your bankruptcy papers as proof. And if your bankruptcy is dismissed or withdrawn, it will still be reported for the same length of time as if you had gone through with it.

Again, while all bankruptcies may be reported for ten years from the date you filed, major credit reporting agencies will remove Chapter 13 bankruptcies seven years from the filing date.

Auto Repossessions

When your car is repo'd, the repossession will be listed on your credit report and remain for seven years from the date of repossession. If you turn in the keys, it's called a voluntary repossession and may appear on your report for the same length of time as a regular repossession, unless you can negotiate something differently with the lender.

Another warning: In most states, your vehicle will be sold at auction and if the price it brings in is less than the balance on the loan (plus legal repossession, attorney or other costs that may apply) you can be sued for the deficiency. A deficiency judgment may then be awarded by the court and also appear on your credit report.

Credit Counseling

While entering a credit counseling program does affect your credit, it may not be as bad as you think. First, most creditors will re-age your accounts once you enter the program and make three on time payments. That means they'll erase those immediate late payments before you entered the program.

For those that do report the account as being paid through credit counseling, the FICO score won't take that into account in calculating your credit score.

Your credit cards, however, will be closed during the program so it will be difficult to get new loans. Also many mortgage lenders will view a credit counseling program as very negative. There are lenders, though, that understand the value of credit counseling and will be willing to finance a loan once you have been successfully paying on your program for at least one or two years, provided you meet their other requirements.

Warning: If the counseling agency pays your creditors late, you will be responsible for those bills and will be stuck with the late payments on your credit report. This has happened, so choose a counseling agency carefully.

Collection Accounts

Collection accounts are tricky and they deserve their own section here. A collection account is automatically considered negative information, so simply paying it may not make a significant difference in your credit score.

There are usually two accounts reported in the case of a collection account: The original account with the lender and the collection account. The exception would be when the original creditor (cell phone company, medical provider etc.) doesn't regularly report to the credit reporting agencies. In those cases, just the collection account will be listed.

If more than one collection account is reported for the same debt because you didn't pay and it was turned over to another collection agency, only the most recent collection account should be listed. Dispute the earlier account.

Details about the original account are much more important than details on the collection account, simply because the collection account is automatically negative. Paying off a collection account, in and of itself, will not likely help your credit score.

If you do have an account that was reported on your credit report – say a major credit card – that was then sent to collections, the original creditor may not be willing to discuss or negotiate with you. If they will, however, it's usually better to work with a creditor than a collection agency.

If the collection account is not paid the creditor or collection agency has a number of years – based on the state statue of limitations – to successfully sue you for the debt. Clearly you don't want a lawsuit on your credit report, but before they sue you, you must be notified they are taking you to court and you may then have an opportunity to negotiate a payoff with then. If the statute of limitations has expired, then you either can't be sued for the debt, or you can raise the statute of limitations as a defense and there's not much they can do to collect from you.

A collection account, as we mentioned earlier, can only be reported seven and a half years from the date you originally missed your payment. Even if you don't pay it, it cannot be reported longer. If a collection agency tells you otherwise, keep notes. Stating that the information can remain longer than it legally can, or that the collector "has ways" to keep it on the report longer could be a violation of the Fair Debt Collection Practices Act which doesn't allow false statements.

Here are some things you should consider as far as your credit report is concerned:

1. Are you likely to get sued for the debt? If so, paying it will prevent a court judgment on your credit report if you lose your case. Of course, it's tough to know when a creditor or collection agency is telling the truth about suing you.

2. Can you get the collection agency to remove the account from your credit file if you pay it off? If they agree, you must get this in writing from them first before you pay. Collection agencies often promise the moon, but don't do a thing once they've been paid. Note: They can't do anything about the account with the original creditor, which may be just as important to your credit.

3. If you negotiate a payoff of less than the full amount, your account listed as "settled" for less than the full amount. Though for a collection account, that's not an issue since it's already negative.

4. Is it an old debt that either can't be reported anymore, or will fall off your credit report soon anyway? Consumers have complained that collection agencies say they'll report debts that are 10 or more years older. That's illegal.

5. What does the original account list? If it lists a charge off with a zero balance, paying if off won't help much. If it lists a charge off with a balance, and by paying it you can get the original creditor to update the account with a zero balance, then you have a chance at boosting your score a little.

If you're applying for a mortgage, the lender may require you to pay off an outstanding collection account before they'll give you a mortgage. Again, aim to get them to remove it if at all possible. If not, at least get something in writing stating it's been paid in full.

Remember, collection agencies are supposed to report the date you first fell behind leading up to the collection account. If yours lists an account and that information isn't included, challenge it.

Your Annual Credit Check Up

Mark your calendar once a year for a credit check up. Go to AnnualCreditReport.com and order free copies of your credit reports from each of the three major credit reporting agencies. I'd go ahead and get them all at once. Since the Big 3 don't share data with each other, you'll want to check them all to make sure they are correct.

If you haven't seen your specialty consumer reports described in Chapter Nine, go ahead and order those as well to make sure there are no surprises.

Visit Credit.com to get a free credit score. You'll learn what's strong about your credit, and what areas need improving. For more information on other services offering free credit scores, see the Resource section.

Next, don't get scammed...

Chapter Seventeen

Scams

A huge irony exists in the marketplace. The more honest Americans there are struggling with poor credit due to divorce, bankruptcy, medical crisis or other life changing event, the more responsible individuals there are who sincerely want to work out their credit issues with integrity and resolve, the more blatant and outrageously fraudulent the scam artists have become in targeting the vulnerable. And the all too frequent result is that a genuine intent to improve one's credit standing is crushed by an unethical operator who only worsens your credit.

How can you avoid being a target for fraud?

First, by reading this chapter and understanding the patterns and come-ons of the scams. The scamsters prey on your fears and vulnerabilities. You need to ask yourself: Am I being manipulated? It is not hard to do. Step back from the come-on and rationally analyze whether it was presented in a way that used your fears to manipulate your decision. Try to see through the come-on. Use your critical thinking skills.

A second way to avoid being a target is to not jump for offers that sound too good to be true. As we all know, what sounds too good probably isn't. The problem is we like the sound of it – "All your credit problems resolved for $199!" or "Guaranteed Credit No Matter What!" The problem's cure has got to be pure cynicism. Don't believe a word of any of it until you completely verify and thoroughly check out the problem. And then still be cynical.

After all, if all of us could have our credit problems resolved for only $199 there would be no need to read this book. Heck, there would be no need to even write this book!

But we're reading and writing because there are no panaceas, there are no simple cures. Credit problems can be overcome when dealt with in a realistic and systematic manner. They are rarely, if ever, cured by paying a third party offering the illusory promise of instant redemption.

The Attorney General in each state deals with credit issues. Assistant attorneys in each state's department work to protect citizens from myriad credit repair scams. It is not an easy job.

Most U.S. states require that credit repair companies register and post a bond with the state's Consumer Affairs Division. Under state law companies may not require the payment of monies in advance of services. And yet such protections are no guarantee. Jo Ann Gibbs, a deputy attorney general for consumer fraud in Las Vegas, Nevada, recounted the case of a credit repair company with a history of legitimate operations. Unfortunately, the company's owner developed a severe gambling addiction and began embezzling the client's money. The fraud was not detected for sometime. When it finally was the consumers were in much worse shape, with even greater debts and late charges now due, than they were before they signed up with the company.

The Nevada Attorney General's office, for example, has investigated a number of companies offering credit repair services for a fee of between $250 and $500. These services only made matters worse for the unsuspecting consumer. The companies would send out a letter to each of the three credit bureaus simply stating that "the debts were not mine" or using only the word "fraud."

The statements were not only incomplete but usually false. Worse yet, by notifying the credit reporting agencies that these consumers may be fraud victims, their accounts are flagged for review and greater security. Those consumers must provide additional information and verification when applying for future credit, and may have more difficulty obtaining credit due to the fraudulent activity reported on their accounts.

Another scam that the Nevada Attorney General's office has investigated involves a credit card come-on for people with bad credit. For a significant amount of money, usually between $299 and $399 (which is directly withdrawn from the consumer's bank account), the scamsters promise a credit card. However, instead of being sent a real credit card, the consumer receives a flimsy pamphlet on credit and an application for a Visa or MasterCard. The consumer is instructed to return the application not to Visa or MasterCard but to the company. The scamsters promise a refund if the consumer's application is rejected for credit three times. This promise is empty and illusory since the application is never actually submitted. Consumer follow up calls are ignored. The bad guys have already banked the money, closed shop, and moved on to bilk more victims.

Allowing the direct withdrawal of monies from your bank account presents its own problems...

Gone Before You Know It

Jim was sitting on the couch beaming and fuming. He was beaming over the fact that he had scored two powerful goals that afternoon at the company soccer game. A few of his more attractive coworkers at the annual picnic were eyeing him favorably for the two unassisted goals he slammed into the back corner of the net. He felt good about that.

He was fuming because he felt worthless. He had fired those goals due to his anger at his financial condition. It seemed like he could never get ahead. Just when everything seemed to be getting better he was doubled up and back on the sidelines.

The latest setback involved his mother and her health. Jim's father had passed away five years ago and hadn't left his mother in the best financial situation. Jim knew his father had intended to do so but there was always another car or vacation or time-share deal to distract him.

Jim's mother had recently had major surgery. She was fine physically but financially the procedure put quite a burden on her. Not wanting her to worry, Jim had taken over the payments. This not only delayed Jim from saving for a house but it severely crimped his monthly budget. He was single and getting older by the day. He wanted to have a family but didn't want to raise children under a financial cloud. And he wasn't getting any nearer to his goal. He had been late on a few bills lately, which greatly bothered him.

Jim figured if he could temporarily get some extra credit all would be fine. And then the phone rang.

The caller asked if Jim would like to qualify for a major credit card. When Jim said he didn't have the best credit the caller said he needn't worry. The card they offered was available regardless of past credit problems.

When Jim indicated an interest the caller promptly asked if he had a checking account. Jim said he did and the caller responded that then they could proceed.

The offer sounded too good to be true. The credit card would allow him some breathing room so he could pay his monthly bills and his mother's medical bills. He felt reasonably positive about getting a raise at work and felt that he could handle the extra payments over the next year.

The caller then asked for information necessary to obtain the new credit card. As Jim answered all the questions the caller asked for him to get one of his checks and to read off all the numbers at the bottom. When Jim asked why this information was needed the caller said it was necessary to help ensure that Jim qualified for this outstanding offer. Jim gave out all the requested information and the caller congratulated him on improving his credit.

Jim hung up the phone and went back to thinking about the coworkers eyeing him that day. If he owned his own place they'd like him even more. Wickedly placed goals were great but a home was an even better goal.

After several weeks Jim wondered what happened to the credit card deal. They were supposed to send him the card within two weeks and he hadn't received anything. He didn't have a number for the company and realized he'd have to wait a while longer.

Two months later Jim received a notice that his checking account was seriously overdrawn. He couldn't understand why. He hadn't spent money on anything but the basics and his mother's medical bills. How could he be overdrawn?

He called the bank to find out what was wrong. The customer service representative indicated that recently a demand draft had been presented for $150 a week.

Jim said he didn't know what a demand draft was and asked for an explanation. The representative informed him that the demand draft had his name, account information and amount on it. Unlike a regular check it didn't require a signature. A total of $750 had been paid to this company. Didn't he know about it?

Jim became angry and wanted to know why the bank would allow someone to pull that much money out of his account without his permission.

The representative politely informed him that they didn't do that, and that by submitting the draft with all of his correct information someone did have his permission. Jim grew angrier and said he had not given any permission to steal money from his account. The representative was calm. She had been through this before. She asked if Jim had given out his checking account information over the phone to anyone.

Jim then remembered the credit card solicitation call. He was curious at the time why the checking account numbers were needed. Now he knew why.

The bank representative was very helpful. She arranged to prevent any further debiting. She gave him the number of their state's Attorney General so he could report the fraud and, perhaps, get his money back if the criminals were ever caught. And she confirmed what Jim now knew: Never give out your bank information over the phone.

The automatic debit scam is alive and well in the country. Unscrupulous telemarketers prey on unsuspecting consumers like Jim everyday. The promises range from credit cards for those with bad credit to valuable prizes for a select group of winners. All that is needed is some basic information, which during the happy gathering period includes confidential checking account information.

A tell tale sign of the scam is when the telemarketer asks in the first minute of the call if you have a checking account. If you don't they will move on to the next potential victim. If you do, they will sell you the sweetest offer to get your information so they can start submitting demand drafts without your signature and raid your account.

Are demand drafts themselves illegal? No. Plenty of people pay their mortgages or their car payments through automatic debiting of their checking account. From a convenience standpoint at the very least it saves a stamp.

But even if you are sure you are working with a reputable company you will want to be careful. Once they have your checking account information, it can be very difficult to cancel the automatic withdrawals. The law allows telemarketers to obtain your authorization to tap your checking account over the phone by obtaining your tape-recorded permission. Do not allow this to happen. Even though the law permits it there is too much room for trickery.

Insist that all permission only be granted in writing and through the mail. Insist that the necessary forms be sent to you. Read them carefully and understand the transaction before you send them back.

And remember to never, ever give out your checking account information over the phone.

Starting Over

Another scam that separates you from your money is as follows:

Gwen and Horace lead an interesting life. Gwen had been born and raised in Rhyl, a small Welsh seaport and vacation spot thirty miles west of Liverpool. Her family knew George Harrison's family when she was growing up and she eventually became friends with all of the Beatles as they were starting out in the small clubs around Liverpool.

Gwen had a mind for numbers. In school she could figure out all of the math problems in less than an instant. As she grew older she could spot mathematic patterns and inconsistencies with amazing alacrity. Her school counselor wanted her to go into science, mathematics or perhaps chartered accounting. But the family needed her in their peewee golf fish and chips enterprise. Naturally, Gwen became the bookkeeper.

Gwen kept up with George and the Beatles as they became worldwide sensations. She'd see them in Liverpool or in Rhyl now and then and was happy for their success. As their band became a business to deal with and their music became an asset to account for the Fab Four complained about the need to keep track of everything. George knew that Gwen had a mind for numbers and asked if she'd come to London to help with the books. Her family realized it was a great opportunity and so Gwen moved to London and started working for the Beatles' Apple Corp. tracking all of the royalty payments.

Royalty statements from publishing and media companies were in the form of hieroglyphics masking misstatements and misrepresentations. They were intentionally vague and difficult to decipher. Ringo wouldn't even look at one. But Gwen learned how to read them and how to challenge them and along the way recovered millions and millions of dollars the band would have otherwise lost. John called her the fifth Beatle.

Gwen met Horace in London during a particularly nasty fight over book royalties. Horace was an American living in England and he represented a larger American publishing house. They had published several Beatle books with great success. The royalties to the band didn't reflect that success. As Gwen tore into their statements Horace became attracted. He had never met such a woman. They were married soon after.

Gwen and Horace settled outside of London. Their respective jobs were challenging and enjoyable and the years passed by quickly. Then one day the two of them realized that they had worked hard enough and it was time to retire. Horace was tired of the grey dampness of England and wanted to move to the sunny climes of Florida. Gwen was game. The two traveled to Tampa to investigate.

A house was located in a nice retirement community. A problem arose as they arranged to purchase it.

Neither Gwen nor Horace had any current established American credit. The banks and the credit bureaus didn't know who they were.

While they had excellent credit in England it didn't travel with them to the United States. They couldn't finance the house.

Gwen made an executive decision. They would sell their house in England and buy the house in Florida with all cash. They would worry about establishing credit later. Horace agreed, the sellers agreed and so it happened.

As they settled into their new house in Florida, Gwen set out to establish credit. She opened a bank account and asked for a credit card. The bank indicated that she had no credit history and would have to start with a debit card, which would not provide a credit reference. Gwen left in a huff. Two other banks said the same thing. Gwen was not pleased.

Later that day she saw a newspaper advertisement for a platinum credit card. The ad promised that participation in the program would lead to a Visa or MasterCard credit card, better credit reports and many other financial benefits. The platinum card cost $99, which given Gwen's frustration level, seemed reasonable to pay. The operator suggested they could automatically debt Gwen's checking account. Gwen didn't like that idea and said she would send a check.

In another week the card arrived and Gwen sensed something was wrong. Her bookkeeping and royalty statement/misstatement antenna was up. The platinum card she paid $99 for only allowed her to make credit purchases from a general merchandise catalog. Plus, the merchandise in the catalog was almost double the price over what a regular discount store charged. If this card was platinum, Gwen fumed, then alchemy existed.

The materials also described how they obtained credit for you. For another $299 a credit card could be obtained. A deposit of $2,000 was required and with that you could charge up to $1,000. The more expensive card was a secured card that only allowed the cardholder to access 50% of the deposit. To get a larger credit line, more money had to be deposited. This wasn't a credit card program, Gwen decided, it was a credit card scam.

Now very angry, Gwen called the number listed to complain. It had a 900 prefix, which Gwen assumed was akin to a toll free 800 line. The line was answered by a recording which indicated that due to call volume she would be on hold for a few minutes. She then heard softened Beatles elevator music, which made Gwen fume even more: Royalties probably weren't being paid.

After an interminable set of songs Gwen finally got a live operator. She demanded to know if this service was a scam. The operator answered her every question with a question, further frustrating Gwen. After a long and circuitous conversation Gwen was able to cancel the service.

On her next phone bill Gwen learned the meaning of a 900 number. She was billed $3.50 a minute for the deliberately elongated 45 minute call. It cost her $157.50 to cancel the platinum card scam service.

Gwen learned the hard way that there was no quick and easy way to establish credit in America. She realized that she would have to establish credit with a variety of local and national credit providers, who over time would help her establish a decent credit profile.

Of course, having an established and readily available credit profile still won't protect you from the myriad of scams out there.

In interviewing the Nevada Attorney General's office for this book, I learned of another common credit scheme: The yo-yo auto loan. Coincidentally, Kristy in our office had been subjected to this "legal" scam only two weeks earlier.

Kristy had always wanted to own a new car. She and her husband Edwin had decided the time was right and began shopping around. On a Saturday they found a great deal on an SUV with low 6% financing. The car dealer said there would be no problem obtaining the loan. "Drive the car home," he said, "your credit is fine." Then on Tuesday the dealer called back with bad news. Their credit wasn't good enough to qualify for the 6% rate. Instead, the best he could do was a 14% rate.

Kristy and Edwin were very upset. They had already driven the new car over 400 miles. The dealer cheerfully informed them they could return the car if they wanted. But did they really want to? Edwin demanded to know how they could sign a contract with credit issues included and then back out of the deal. The dealer pleasantly noted that the contract allowed the dealer to rescind the transaction within 15 days if the right credit wasn't arranged. As a favor to them, when the 6% financing fell through, he went and found the 14% financing.

For Kristy the ploy was pure manipulation. The car was already hers. It handled well and was fun to drive. The last thing she wanted to do was turn it back in. She and Edwin grudgingly accepted the new higher financing.

Neil Rombardo served with the Nevada Attorney General's office in Carson City and dealt with yo-yo auto loan schemes. Rombardo explained that the scheme is "legal" since the contract allows the dealer to terminate for a failure to find acceptable credit, and state law does not prohibit such transactions. Interestingly, while the dealer can terminate within 15 days under state law, the buyer cannot.

Rombardo noted that while most consumers will reluctantly accept the new financing, a few have been angry enough to take the car back. Tellingly (and not surprisingly) the next day dealers have called these consumers back to say they have miraculously arranged for the original lower financing that was sought. The car is theirs.

To avoid the yo-yo auto loan scam, be sure to line up auto financing with your bank or credit union before you go shopping for a new car. If for some reason you are faced with this scam, report the dealers to your state's Consumer Affairs Division.

Identity Theft

Just as there are many organized groups – from nationally advertised credit card scamsters to unscrupulous local car dealers – systematically taking advantage of consumers, there are individuals at work trying to steal your very identity and the good credit that comes with it.

Identity theft is a very personal scam. And it can arise from the people close to you.

Jeffrey had a drug problem. He tried not to let anyone around him become aware of it. But he was addicted to cocaine and his very close friends and family members all knew it. They couldn't ignore the very obvious signs, the hollowed out cheeks and eyes, the slight twitch in his hands and the ever constant sniffling.

Jeffrey was a big man used to getting his way. He was the oldest of three brothers and knew how to bully his way forward. He had used cocaine recreationally with friends in college. All had agreed in those days that it was a good social drug, and there were plenty of women attracted to Jeffery because he carried a party night's worth of cocaine. Jeffrey felt alive on cocaine. Always a talker, he had a heightened sense of communicative ability while he was on the drug

But Jeffrey's friends had moved on. They had all felt the negative effects of the misnamed 'good drug'. They were seeing the wreckage cocaine inflicted upon their friends. They were seeing lives wasted away.

Jeffrey was in too deep. He couldn't pull back, and found himself in a downward spiral of needing even more money for his terrible habit and becoming ever less employable for his terrible habit.

No one ever confronted Jeffrey. He was always used to getting his way and talking his way out of any spot. His family was unprepared to deal with such a problem, and could only hope that he would pull out of it. His friends, tired of being hit up for money that was never repaid, tended to drift away. Jeffrey was becoming more and more isolated at a time he needed the most help.

Jeffery's most recent job was an insurance claims representative. He could talk to people on the phone. His customers never knew he had a problem. They never saw him in person, and never spoke to him long enough to know the sad truth about Jeffrey.

But Jeffrey's co-workers soon found out.

The claim's representative job didn't quite pay Jeffrey enough. He had an expensive cocaine habit that came before rent, food or any of the other lesser necessities. He needed to make ends meet.

Jeffrey learned that many of the claims reps did personal business on their computers at work. Some did stock trading for their own brokerage accounts while the stock market was open during business hours. A few of the traders were always joking with each other in the break room over their latest hits and misses.

Jeffrey stayed late one day after work. He was in desperate need of money for another few ounces of cocaine. He rationalized that the traders were cheating the company out of work time by doing such personal business. He was justified in his next step. When everyone was gone Jeffrey got onto one the claim rep's computers. It was very easy to get into the brokerage account. It was one click away from their favorites page. The computer was set to remember personal passwords automatically. He worked quickly on the first machine and then rapidly moved to the next cubicle. In less than ten minutes Jeffrey was armed with the sensitive brokerage information for three of his co-workers accounts. He immediately went home and went to work on his home computer. Within an hour Jeffery was able to cash out the brokerage accounts from the comfort of his home. He was flying high on excellent cocaine before any of his co-workers knew what hit them.

Jeffrey liked the ease of this type of fund raising. Like the tens of thousands of other addicts, low lifes and assorted black hearts, Jeffrey became an "IDBG", an identity bad guy, and started looking for other opportunities. On one of the few occasions he was invited to a family function he was parking in front of his uncle's modest house as the mail was being delivered. Being the thoughtful nephew, he carried the mail into the house. Then he noticed that his uncle had received a box of new checks in the mail from the bank. Jeffrey sensed a fund raising opportunity and without anyone noticing threw the box of checks into the trunk of his car.

After the family gathering Jeffrey set about satisfying his habit. Through a friend of his drug dealer he had been introduced to a man who manufactured false identification cards. It was a booming market with all the IDBG's getting into the business. It was extremely easy for Jeffrey to have an ID made featuring the uncle's information combined with Jeffrey's photo. With the fake ID and the real checks Jeffrey was able to drain his uncle's account by writing checks for cash at a nearby Indian casino.

The sudden loss of money from his checking account caused Jeffrey's uncle a severe amount of financial strain. He almost lost his house to foreclosure and was assessed with a massive amount of late fees on the multitude of bounced checks. The family was furious. By the handwriting on the checks they knew it was Jeffrey's work.

It was at this point that the family finally confronted Jeffrey's drug problem. They weren't going to spend a lot of money on a fancy addiction clinic for Jeffrey. They did it old school. Using chloroform to knock him out, Jeffrey's two younger brothers transported him to one of their basements. He was handcuffed to a leash from the wall where he could access a bed and a toilet. His cocaine withdrawal was not pretty or pleasant. But after what he had done to his uncle, no one cared about the deserving pain he went through.

When it was over Jeffrey was clean. For how long no one knew.

Identity theft is often called the fastest growing crime in America. There's a good chance that you or someone you love will have your personal information compromised, and possibly used to apply for credit or even medical benefits under your name. Even more frightening: Children and students at college are falling victim at increasing rate. In the case of children, family members who have bad credit may use their children's information to get credit or utility services. If the bills aren't paid on time, however, the child pays the price with bad credit. In the case of college students, the fact that they are often living with roommates and moving frequently makes it very easy for someone else to assume their information and get credit cards or other types of credit.

Most identity theft victims find out about it in a negative manner. For example, they apply for credit and are turned down based on negative information in their credit files. Or they receive a call from a debt collector about a bill about which they know nothing.

Given the enormity of the problem it is important for everyone to know how to avoid becoming a victim of identity theft. The following eleven tips may keep you from becoming the next statistic.

1. Jealously guard your Social Security Number. This one number can give the wrong person the keys to your castle. Avoid giving it out over the phone. Know that California has a state law which prohibits many businesses from requiring your Social Security Number. If the national company wants your number tell them they are violating California law (even if you live in Texas). Do not carry your social security card with you. Keep it in a safe deposit box or other secure place.

2. Sign your credit cards as soon as you receive them. It is harder for a criminal to obtain merchandise when your signature is on the card. It is easy for an IDBG to sign your card, get the necessary back up identification and have a field day with your credit and your identity.

3. Even if you are the most forgetful person on earth do not attach your Social Security Number or personal identification number (PIN) to any card you carry with you. In fact, it would be best if you forgot to do that altogether. If you lose that card or it is stolen having those numbers attached will make life easy for an IDBG, and make your life miserable for a while, or even longer.

4. Similarly, don't write your PIN or social on an invoice or receipt that may be thrown away. You'd be surprised at who is rifling through the trash: Some trashy people.

5. Check your receipts to make sure you received yours and not someone else's information. The "someone else" may misuse what they just received.

6. Don't give out any confidential information or account numbers to anyone unless you are certain that they are worthy of it. And even then think twice about giving it out. As our cases have illustrated there are many innocent sounding requests made of you by people last innocent in grade school.

7. Put difficult and unique passwords on your bank accounts, credit cards and personal accounts. Don't use standard, predictable and easy to obtain information like a mother's maiden name or a birth date as a password. Please do not use "1,2,3,4," which series of numbers accounts for a staggeringly large number of passwords. Consider instead using cool and obscure Australian place names such as Yarrawonga, Mullumbimby or Wagga Wagga. Get out the atlas and have some fun. (If the IDBG after you is an all knowing aborigine your luck may have already run out.)

8. Be careful on the road. Business travelers are especially vulnerable to identity theft because they rely on electronic devices that can be easily lost or hacked. And wireless networks at hotels and airports are feeding grounds for sophisticated hackers.

9. If you don't receive your regular statements in the mail contact the creditor immediately. Someone may be stealing your mail. As well, if your mail is not dropped through a slot into your house but rather left outside in an exposed mailbox you may want to reconsider where you receive your mail. An option is to have creditor statements and confidential mailings directed to a secure mail receiving service.

10. Check your credit report on a regular basis for signs of improper account activity, new and unknown account openings and other warning signs. Be proactive in protecting your credit and your identity.

11. Buy a shredder. Then use it.

By taking these steps you will reduce your chances of becoming the next identity theft victim. Nevertheless, for all your proactive steps, it still may happen and you need to know what to do.

The Federal Trade Commission has been actively involved in the problems of identity theft. The FTC suggests promptly taking the following three steps:

1. Notify the fraud departments at Experian, TransUnion and Equifax that you are an identity theft victim. You can either "freeze" your credit – which prevents your information from being used unless the file is "unfrozen" with a PIN, or request that a 'fraud alert' be placed in your file which alerts creditors to be extra careful before extending credit. If you know you are a victim of fraud, a freeze is appropriate. If you are simply worried because your wallet has gone missing, a fraud alert may be the next appropriate step.

2. Call all your creditors, including utilities, the phone company, credit card companies and the like, and ask to speak to a representative in the fraud (or security) department. Find out if any existing accounts have been tampered with or if any new accounts have been improperly opened. Close any account that has been tampered with and then open a new account with a unique Australian place named password.

3. File a police report in your home town and, if applicable, in the city where the identity theft occurred. While we all know how useful filing a police report can be ("Oh, I see this isn't a drug case. We'll get back to you.") in one civil case out of a thousand the local authorities actually do something. You might be the lucky one. Plus, creditors may require the report if you report unauthorized use of your accounts or information.

4. Monitor your credit reports for unusual activity. This is an example of a situation where paying for a credit monitoring service that monitors your information with all three of the major credit reporting agencies would be worth it.

As mentioned, the FTC is very interested in this large and growing problem. They maintain a special Identity Theft Hotline at 1-877-IDTHEFT (1-877-438-4338). You can also file a complaint online at consumer.gov/idtheft. You'll find more helpful ID theft prevention information at IdentityTheft911.com.

Finally, put it all together to be a credit winner...

Chapter Eighteen

Winning With Credit

We've reviewed a lot of information about how the credit system works. Now it's time to put it all together. There are several basic principles to using good debt to your advantage. Learning these will be a critical part of becoming financially independent.

#1: Have a positive goal. Getting out of debt by and large is a negative goal. It implies you don't want something: Debt. But building wealth is a positive goal. That's much more motivating. So while you are creating your plan to get out of debt, at the same time figure out how that will free up cash flow for you to devote to your positive wealth-building goals. Keep your eye on the real prize.

#2: Live rich, even if you aren't. Robert Kiyosaki's Rich Dad never said he should be cheap to reach his goals. In fact, he told Robert that he didn't understand people who were too cheap. "You can become rich by being cheap. But the problem is, even though you're rich you're still cheap." Instead he advised Robert to find out what he wanted, learn the price, and then decide if he wanted to pay the price.

Getting out of debt will teach you a lot about yourself. When your ultimate goal, creating wealth, becomes more important than the stuff you're wasting money on, you'll find the way.

Read books on becoming wealthy. Start a mastermind group. Immerse yourself in thoughts about what you're working toward so you can stop focusing on the negatives of your current situation. Learning from people wealthier than you will help you set your sights much higher than you have already.

#3: Know when to cut your losses. Bad things happen to good people. Responsible, caring people get sick, lose their jobs, get divorced and even file for bankruptcy. At some point you have to decide to cut your losses and start moving forward. It's tragic to see people wiping out what little wealth they've squirreled away in their retirement funds in a last ditch to pay their credit card bill or save their credit rating. It's terrible to see people lose their homes to foreclosure because they aren't willing to face the reality of their situation.

Many of the top financial successes in this country have been through personal failure, including bankruptcy. They went on to create personal fortunes and contribute to worthy causes. Whether it's filing for bankruptcy, entering a debt negotiation program or selling your home through a short sale to avoid foreclosure, if you're in a crisis, do what you need to do and then start moving forward again.

#4: Get smart about credit. Start reading the fine print on your credit card statements and cardholder agreements. Get savvy about shopping for lower rates. Find explanations for terms you don't understand. The money you save can be used to make you many more dollars in the future.

#5: Know the difference between good debt and bad debt. Good debt helps you leverage your financial life to create wealth-producing assets. Bad debt sucks your money away because you end up spending much more for the things you buy, many of which are gone by the time you pay the bill. Before you take on new debt, ask yourself whether it is really good debt or bad debt.

#6: Learn about business credit. This book is about personal credit, though many of the topics apply to business owners as well. But there is another world of business credit that involves business credit reports, other reporting agencies such as D&B, and special strategies and nuances. If you are a business owner, or plan to be, my book *Business Credit Success: Get On The Financial Fast Track* will show you how.

Conclusion

As we have learned throughout this book, you can get out of debt and win with credit. Millions of Americans have done it before you, and hopefully you will be one of the many millions who will do so in the future.

With a positive goal, a clear idea of the difference between good debt and bad debt and by taking advantage of the Resources in the following section you too can win.

Good Luck.

Appendix A

Sample Letters

Sample Letter to Collection Agency
Requesting Verification of Debt

Your name and address

Date

Name and address of collection agency

RE: Account number (list account number if given)

Dear Sir or Madam,

I was recently informed that I owe a debt in the amount of $(list amount of debt).

I don't believe that debt is correct (or I don't know what this debt is for, etc.). Please send me written verification of the debt.

Sincerely,

Your name

Sample Letter to Debt Collector Requesting They Stop Contacting You

Your name and address

Date

Name and address of collection agency

RE: Account number (list account number if given)

Dear Sir or Madam,

I have been in contact with your agency about a debt in the amount of $(list amount of debt) to (list original creditor).

I ask you to stop contacting me about that debt. (You may choose to give a reason: As I have stated I don't believe I owe it, I cannot pay any portion of the debt at this time, I believe it's too old to be collected, etc.)

Thank you,

Your name

Sample Letter to Debt Collector For Settlement of Debt

Your name and address

Date

Name and address of collection agency

RE: Account number (list account number if given)

Dear Sir or Madam,

I have been in contact with your agency about a debt in the amount of $(list amount of debt) to (list original creditor).

Today we agreed that if I pay $(amount of settled debt) that this debt will be settled in full. You will promptly notify the creditor that there is no balance due on the debt. You will also promptly notify the credit reporting agencies (either that the debt has been settled with no balance due, or that it will be removed from the credit bureau records).

When I receive your written confirmation of these terms of our agreement, I will make the payment we agreed upon.

Sincerely,

Your name

Sample Letter to Debt Collector For Payment Arrangement

Your name and address

Date

Name and address of collection agency

RE: Account number (list account number if given)

Dear (name of collector you've been dealing with),

I have been in contact with your agency about a debt in the amount of $(list amount of debt) to (list original creditor).

As we have discussed, I am making every effort to pay this debt as quickly as I can given my current financial situation.

We have agreed that I will pay $(dollar amount) on a $(monthly, weekly or other) basis. I have included the first check (or money order) based on our agreement today. If this is not our agreement, please return the enclosed check and contact me to discuss other arrangements.

Thank you,

Your name

Sample Letter to Credit Reporting Agency Disputing Wrong Information

Note: handwrite your dispute if your handwriting is legible

Your name and address

Last four digits of your social security number

Your credit report number

Date

Name and address of credit reporting agency

Dear Sir or Madam,

I am disputing the following account listed on my credit report:
(List account details)
It (choose one of the following or modify for your needs: is not my account, is too old to legally be reported, has an incorrect balance, was never late, has been paid in full, etc.)
Please investigate and reply as soon as possible.

Thank you,

Your name

Sample Letter to Lender Disputing Wrong Information on Credit Report

Note: handwrite your dispute if your handwriting is easy to read.

Your name and address

Your social security number

Your account number (if available)

Date

Name and address of lender or furnisher

Dear Sir or Madam,

I am disputing the following account listed on my (Experian, Equifax, and/or TransUnion) credit report:

(List account details)

It (choose one of the following or modify for your needs: is not my account, is too old to legally be reported, has an incorrect balance, was never late, is paid in full, etc.)

Please investigate and reply as soon as possible.

Thank you,

Your name

Appendix B

Worksheets

Worksheet for Tracking Spending

Spending Item	Amount Budgeted	Actual
Monthly Income		
Source:		
Source:		
Source:		
Total Income:		
Taxes		
Federal		
State		
Personal property		
Other:		
Total Taxes:		
Housing		
Mortgage or rent		
Property taxes		
Homeowner/Renter insurance		
Electric		
Gas or oil		
Water		
Trash collection		
Other utilities		
Association/Condo fees		
Landscaping		
Cleaning		
Maintenance/Repairs		

Alarm system		
Telephone – local service		
Telephone – long distance		
Cell phone		
Other:		
Other:		
Total housing:		
Automobile (boat, or motorcycle)		
Payment auto 1		
Gas auto 1		
Maintenance auto 1		
Repair auto 1		
Payment auto 2		
Gas auto 2		
Maintenance auto 2		
Repair auto 2		
Payment auto 3		
Gas auto 3		
Maintenance 3		
Repair auto 3		
Parking		
Public transportation		
Other		
Other		
Total auto		
Food		
Groceries		
Lunch/meals at work		
Snacks		
Kid lunches		
Pizza delivery/carryout		
Fast food		
Meals out		
Coffee/beverages		
Other:		
Other:		
Total Food		
Education		
Tuition		
Books		
Supplies		
Other:		

Other:		
Total Education		
Health		
Doctor visits/copays		
Wellness services		
Prescription medicine		
Over-the-counter medicine		
Dentist		
Vision (including glasses/contacts)		
Supplements		
Other:		
Total Health		
Entertainment		
Movies/Concerts		
Movie rentals		
Cable TV		
Internet service		
Sporting events		
Books		
Magazine subscriptions		
CDs/Music		
Birthday parties		
Holiday parties		
Other:		
Other:		
Total Entertainment		
Insurance		
Disability		
Life		
Credit		
Auto		
Health		
Homeowner		
Private mortgage insurance		
Umbrella policy		
Boat Insurance		
Extended warranty		
Other:		
Total Insurance		
Pets		
Food		

Medical		
Supplies		
Grooming		
Other:		
Total Pets		
Clothing		
Professional attire		
Leisure attire		
Hosiery/socks		
Underwear/lingerie		
Shoes/Accessories		
Jewelry		
Dry cleaning/Alterations		
Total Clothing		
Personal Care		
Haircuts/Perms/Coloring		
Manicure/Pedicure/Waxing		
Gym membership/Exercise classes		
Makeup		
Toiletries		
Other:		
Other:		
Total Personal Care		
Child Care		
Day-care/Tuition		
Extracurricular		
Baby-sitting		
Toys		
Gifts		
Summer camp		
Clothing		
Allowance		
Other:		
Other:		
Total Child Care		
Vacations		
Airfare/Gas		
Lodging		
Food		
Souvenirs		
Gifts		

Other:		
Other:		
Total Vacation		
Holidays		
Gifts		
Decorating		
Entertainment		
Other:		
Other:		
Charitable		
Church/Synagogue/House of worship		
Other:		
Other:		
Other:		
Total Charitable		
Miscellaneous		
Cigarettes		
Hobby		
Other:		
Other:		
Other:		
Other:		
Total Miscellaneous		

Source: Ultimate Credit Solutions Inc. Reprinted with permission

Debt Worksheet

Creditor	Good Debt?	APR %	New APR	Balance	Minimum payment

Total Monthly Debt Payment: _____

How to Use This Worksheet

Make a copy of this chart since you will have to update it periodically.

Creditor: List each creditor in the first column.

Good debt or bad debt? Write "Good" next to the debt that is good debt, "Bad" to the debt that is bad debt. Paying off bad debt is your priority.

APR: Next list the interest rate. If your credit card has balances with different interest rates, an effective interest rate should be listed. Use that here.

New APR: When you call to negotiate a lower interest rate, note the rate the issuer will give you here. If you can't successfully negotiate, simply use a check mark so you at least know you've tried. Try again once you pay some balances down.

Balance: List your current balance. On bad debts, stop charging.

Minimum Payment: List the required minimum payment here.

Once you have completed this list, decide which debt elimination strategy you prefer to use: 1) eliminating the high-interest bad debt first to save the most in interest payments over the life of these debts; or 2) Robert and Kim Kiyosaki's method of first paying off the debt with the lowest total balance to quickly give yourself success in your debt elimination plan (see Chapter 4). Now highlight the target debt you'll be paying off first. When you have paid that one off, target the next bad debt on your list and pay that one off, and so on until you become debt-free. Now start building wealth.

Appendix C

Resources

Resources For Success

Visit CorporateDirect.com/credit for updated resources to help implement the advice given in this book.

Build Business Credit

Learn how to establish a strong business credit history and build a winning strategy for your business' financing needs. Read *Business Credit Success: Get On The Financing Fast Track*. It will show you how.

Counseling

Credit Counseling Service: For a referral to a credit counseling agency, visit CorporateDirect.com/credit.

Debtors Anonymous: Operated under the same principles as Alcoholics Anonymous, DA helps chronic debtors stop debting. To find if there is a group in your area, or for more information, write: Debtors Anonymous, General Service Office, P.O. Box 920888, Needham, MA 02492-0009. Ph: 781-453-2743; Fax: 781-453-2745; or visit debtorsanonymous.org.

Debt Negotiation and Settlement: For a referral to a debt negotiation and settlement firm, visit CorporateDirect.com/credit.

Financial Recovery Institute: Financial Recovery™ Counseling is a structured process that helps clients transform their relationship with money. It seeks to treat the "whole person," including addressing the client's history with, and emotions relating to, money. Visit financialrecovery.com.

Housing Help: For a referral to a company that can help you with options for a mortgage you can't afford, or to refinance a property with little or no equity, visit CorporateDirect.com/credit.

Credit Reporting Agencies

You can order a copy of your credit report from each national credit reporting agency once a year at AnnualCreditReport.com.

Debt Collectors

Debt Collection Answers: How to Use Debt Collection Laws to Protect Your Rights is an ebook written by consumer educators Gerri Detweiler and Mary Reed. Visit DebtCollectionAnswers.com for more information.

Debt Blaster

You can obtain a copy of the Debt Blaster software through CorporateDirect.com.

Government Agencies

Consumer Financial Protection Bureau (CFPB) regulates many financial services products and enforces consumer financial protection regulations. Visit ConsumerFinance.gov.

Federal Trade Commission: Contact the FTC at FTC.gov or 1-877-FTC-HELP for help with Internet, telemarketing, identity theft or other fraud complaints. Use their extensive website for consumer information brochures, or to read copies of consumer protection laws.

Kids and Money

Financial literacy is a vital skill for kids, but most learn through the school of hard knocks. Visit jumpstart.org to learn how you can help support financial literacy education.

Radio

Listen to Talk Credit Radio at GerriDetweiler.com for current information on credit and debt strategies.

Student Loans

The Department of Education's ombudsman service may provide assistance if you have exhausted all your options and cannot pay your student loan at Ombudsman.ed.gov.

Finaid.org and StudentLoanBorrowerAssistance.org offer excellent information about student loans, including options if you default.

ForgiveStudentLoanDebt.com and StudentLoanJustice.org are grassroots initiatives that are bringing national attention to the issue of student loan debt problems.

IBRinfo.org offers helpful calculators and tools to help you learn whether you are eligible for the income-based repayment program.

The Project on Student Debt is an initiative of the Institute for College Access & Success, a nonprofit independent research and policy organization dedicated to making college more available and affordable to people of all backgrounds. Projectonstudentdebt.org.

Websites

Following are some additional helpful websites. For updates and new additions, visit CorporateDirect.com/credit for updates.

CallforAction.org is an international non-profit network of consumer hotlines affiliated with local broadcast partners. Volunteer professionals assist consumers through mediation and education to help resolve problems with businesses and government agencies.

CardRatings.com: Provides free information on low-rate, secured and other credit cards.

Consumer-Action.org: You'll get a free list of secured cards, a list of low-rate credit cards, and a variety of other helpful publications in many languages. (Note, you must include the hyphen between the words "consumer" and "action" to get to the correct site.)

ConsumerFed.org: The Consumer Federation of America lobbies for consumers' rights and also offers booklets on saving money, buying a home, managing debts, resolving consumer complaints, etc.

ConsumerWorld.org is a very comprehensive site with lots of helpful consumer money-saving information.

Credit.com is a free website that will help you shop for a credit card, monitor your credit reports and scores, and find answers to many of your credit questions.

DebtConsolidationCare.com is the web's first get out of debt community. Experienced moderators help answer thousands of questions from community members working their way out of debt, and they do it for free.

FinancialRecovery.com: Need one-on-one help to conquer your debt or get your finances on track? The Financial Recovery Institute can refer you to a trained counselor. This is not financial planning or credit counseling, but instead fills the gap between the two.

Fraud.org: Home of the National Fraud Information Center, which gives consumers the information they need to avoid becoming victims of telemarketing and Internet fraud and to help them get their complaints to law enforcement agencies quickly and easily. If you suspect telemarketing or Internet fraud, visit their website immediately to file a complaint form.

GerriDetweiler.com features free podcasts on a variety of credit topics by radio host and credit expert Gerri Detweiler. (She is also a contributor to this book.)

GetOutOfDebt.org is run by Steve Rhode, who used to run a large, successful credit counseling agency. He helps people for free by highlighting debt scams and answering questions about options for dealing with debt.

NCLC.org. The National Consumer Law Center publishes helpful books and legal manuals for consumer law attorneys as well as counselors who help consumers. Their book, Surviving Debt, is a useful guide if you are having serious financial problems.

Stretcher.org. The Dollar Stretcher offers a wealth of money-saving information, and is one of the original websites focused on savvy "penny pinching" strategies.

TheCollegeSolution.com offers advice for parents and students who want to avoid racking up huge education debt.

AskLizWeston.com features advice from the web's #1 personal finance writer Liz Weston. She is also the author of *Your Credit Score: How to Improve the 3-Digit Number That Shapes Your Financial Future.*

DebtProofLiving.com is a community offering support and tools to get out of debt. Founded by Mary Hunt who herself paid off $100,000 in credit card debt.

For an up-to-date list of helpful websites, visit CorporateDirect.com/credit.

PROMISSORY NOTE*

$[AMOUNT]
[DATE OF NOTE]

For value received, [Name of Promisor], (hereinafter the "Promisor"), an individual [OR a [State of Incorporation,]] corporation, promises to pay upon demand to [Name of individual or company loaning money], of [address of individual or company loaning the money] (hereinafter the "Promisee"), the principal sum of [Amount being loaned] of lawful money of the United States of America on the date that is [Due Date, in months/weeks, etc.] from the date of this Promissory Note, [OPTIONAL together with interest on the principal sum set out above at the rate of ___% per annum, compounded annually.] The Promisor, reserves the right to prepay without penalty.

As security for the repayment of this Promissory Note the Promisor agrees to grant to the Promisee a lien over all of the real and personal property now or hereafter belonging to the Promisor [Or such other security as is being put up as collateral for the loan]. At the request of the Promisee the Promisor shall also provide evidence of such lien in a form registerable under the Uniform Commercial Code.

All remedies hereunder or by law afforded shall be cumulative and all shall be available to the Promisee in connection with this Note until the liability of the Promisor herein created has been paid in full. In the event of any dispute, the prevailing party shall be entitled to attorneys fees and costs. Exclusive venue shall be the [District, County, State, etc.].

IN WITNESS WHEREOF, the Promisor has executed this Note the day and year first above written.

PROMISOR

_____

Signature

*This is a sample note. It is suggested you seek the counsel of an attorney when preparing such documents.

Index

About the Author

Garrett Sutton, Esq., is the bestselling author of *Start Your Own Corporation, Run Your Own Corporation, The ABC's of Getting Out of Debt, Writing Winning Business Plans, Buying and Selling a Business* and *The Loopholes of Real Estate* in Robert Kiyosaki's Rich Dad's Advisors series. Garrett has over thirty years' experience in assisting individuals and businesses to determine their appropriate corporate structure, limit their liability,  protect their assets and advance their financial, personal and credit success goals.

Garrett and his law firm, Sutton Law Center, have offices in Reno, Nevada, Jackson Hole, Wyoming and Rocklin, California. The firm represents many corporations, limited liability companies, limited partnerships and individuals in their real estate and business-related law matters, including incorporations, contracts, and ongoing business-related legal advice. The firm continues to accept new clients.

Garrett is also the owner of Corporate Direct, which since 1988 has provided affordable asset protection and corporate formation services. He is the author of *How to Use Limited Liability Companies and Limited Partnerships*, which further educates readers on the proper use of entities. Along with credit expert Gerri Detweiler, Garrett also assists entrepreneurs build business credit. Please see CorporateDirect.com for more information.

Garrett attended Colorado College and the University of California at Berkeley, where he received a B.S. in Business Administration in 1975. He graduated with a J.D. in 1978 from Hastings College of Law, the University of California's law school in San Francisco. He practiced law in San Francisco and Washington, D.C. before moving to Reno and the proximity of Lake Tahoe.

Garrett is a member of the State Bar of Nevada, the State Bar of California, and the American Bar Association. He has written numerous professional articles and has served on the Publication Committee of the State Bar of Nevada. He has appeared in the *Wall Street Journal, The New York Times* and other publications.

Garrett enjoys speaking with entrepreneurs and real estate investors on the advantages of forming business entities. He is a frequent lecturer for small business groups as well as the Rich Dad's Advisors series.

Garrett serves on the boards of the American Baseball Foundation, located in Birmingham, Alabama, and the Sierra Kids Foundation and Nevada Museum of Art, both based in Reno.

For more information on Garrett Sutton and Sutton Law Center, please visit his Web sites at www.sutlaw.com, www.corporatedirect.com, and www.successdna.com.

References and Resources

For additional information, the following websites are suggested:

Books and Information for Investors and Entrepreneurs
www.BZKPress.com

Real Estate
www.Ken.Mcelroy.com

www.mccompanies.com

Asset Protection and LLC Formation
www.sutlaw.com

www.corporatedirect.com

Tax Planning
www.TaxFreeWealthBook.com

Sales Strategies
www.salesdogs.com

The Rich Dad Company
www.RichDad.com

Notes

Other Books by
Garrett Sutton, Esq.

Start Your Own Corporation
Why the Rich Own their Own Companies and Everyone Else Works for Them

Writing Winning Business Plans
How to Prepare a Business Plan that Investors Will Want to Read – and Invest In

Buying and Selling a Business
How You Can Win in the Business Quadrant

The ABCs of Getting Out of Debt
Turn Bad Debt into Good Debt and Bad Credit into Good Credit

Run Your Own Corporation
How to Legally Operate and Properly Maintain Your Company into the Future

The Loopholes of Real Estate
Secrets of Successful Real Estate Investing

• • • • • • • • • • • • •

How to Use Limited Liability Companies & Limited Partnerships
Getting the Most Out of Your Legal Structure
(a SuccessDNA book)

Bulletproof Your Corporation, Limited Liability Company and Limited Partnership
How to Raise and Maintain the Corporate Veil of Protection
(a Corporate Direct book)

Start a Business Toolbox
A Complete Resource for New Entrepreneurs
(a Corporate Direct book)

For more information about Garrett Sutton and his law firm visit www.sutlaw.com.

For more free entrepreneur information and resources visit www.successdna.com.

Notes

RICH DAD

ADVISORS

The Rich Dad Advisors series of books was created to deliver the how-to content to support Robert Kiyosaki's series of international bestsellers: *Rich Dad Poor Dad* and the Rich Dad series of books. In *Rich Dad Poor Dad*—the #1 Personal Finance Book of all Time—Robert presented the foundation for the Rich Dad principles and philosophies and set the stage for his context-changing messages that have changed the way the world thinks about money, business and investing.

The Rich Dad Advisors series of books has sold more than 2 million copies worldwide and BKZ Press, exclusive publisher of the Rich Dad Advisor series and the licensor of International Rights for the series, will be releasing several new titles that will expand both the scope and depth of the series.

Rich Dad Poor Dad represents the most successful book on personal finance in our generation. Over the last 15 years, its messages have inspired millions of people and impacted tens of millions of lives in over 100 countries around the world. The Rich Dad books have continued to stay on the international bestseller lists because their messages continue to resonate with readers of all ages. *Rich Dad Poor Dad* has succeeded in lifting the veil of confusion, fear, and frustration around money and replacing it with clarity, truth, and hope for every person who is willing to commit to the process of becoming financially educated.

In order to make good on the promise of financial literacy and ultimate freedom, Robert Kiyosaki assembled his own team of personal and trusted advisors, proven experts in their respective fields, to deliver the only complete 'how-to' series of books and programs that takes the messages of Rich Dad to the streets of the world and gives each reader the step-by-step processes to achieve wealth and income in business, investing, and entrepreneurship.

BZK Press is driven by several of Kiyosaki's actual Advisors who have committed to take the messages of Rich Dad, convert them to practical applications and make sure those processes are put in the hands of those who seek financial literacy and financial freedom around the world. The series gives practical, proven processes to succeed in the areas of finance, tax, entrepreneurship, investing, property, debt, sales, wealth management and both business and personal development. Three of these trusted and accomplished Advisors—Blair Singer, Garrett Sutton, and Ken McElroy— are the driving forces behind BZK Press.

BZK Press is proud to assume the role of publisher of the Rich Dad Advisor series and perpetuate a series of books that has sold millions of copies worldwide and, more importantly, supported tens of millions in their journey toward financial freedom.

Best-Selling Books
in the Rich Dad Advisors Series

by Blair Singer

SalesDogs
You Don't Have to Be an Attack Dog to Explode Your Income

Team Code of Honor
The Secrets of Champions in Business and in Life

by Garrett Sutton, Esq.

Start Your Own Corporation
Why the Rich Own Their Own Companies and Everyone Else Works for Them

Writing Winning Business Plans
How to Prepare a Business Plan that Investors will Want to Read – and Invest In

Buying and Selling a Business
How You Can Win in the Business Quadrant

The ABCs of Getting Out of Debt
Turn Bad Debt into Good Debt and Bad Credit into Good Credit

Run Your Own Corporation
How to Legally Operate and Properly Maintain Your Company into the Future

by Ken McElroy

The ABCs of Real Estate Investing
The Secrets of Finding Hidden Profits Most Investors Miss

The ABCs of Property Management
What You Need to Know to Maximize Your Money Now

The Advanced Guide to Real Estate Investing
How to Identify the Hottest Markets and Secure the Best Deals

by Tom Wheelwright

Tax-Free Wealth
How to Build Massive Wealth by Permanently Lowering Your Taxes